DE

BREAKING THE TABOO

DEATH
BREAKING THE TABOO

INTERVIEWS BY
ANNA HOWARD

ARTHUR JAMES
EVESHAM

First published in 1996 by

ARTHUR JAMES LTD
4 Broadway Road
Evesham
Worcestershire WR11 6BH

ISBN 0 85305 343 3

Typeset in Adobe Garamond by
Strathmore Publishing Services, London N7

Printed in Great Britain by
The Guernsey Press Company Ltd, Guernsey, C.I.

In memory of

ANN BENFIELD

Acknowledgements

There are many people I would like to thank for their help and guidance in the creation of this book. I owe the most profound thanks of all to the people I interviewed: for their time, for their generosity and trust in revealing some of their most private thoughts and feelings, and for their willingness to share these with an unknown audience.

I am eternally grateful to Shirley du Boulay, my friend and mentor. She listened to my ideas and helped me shape them, contributed several of her own, introduced me to my publisher and helped me keep my feet on the ground.

I would like to thank Judith Longman for her enthusiastic support, her sensitivity and her professional eye for detail and structure. John Bright, Juliet Johnson and all the staff at BBC Radio Oxford who trained me and gave unprecedented personal support. Brian and Nancy Walker for giving me a week of silence and solitude in Wales at the very beginning of this project. Professor Mike World; Tim Newell, Governor of HMP Grendon; the Bristol Cancer Help Centre; the Rt Revd Richard Harries, Bishop of Oxford; Mother Frances Dominica; Revd Andrew Cain and Brian Keenan – for moral support.

There are certain friends whose background encouragement I have valued greatly: Jenny Steel, Martine Planchais, Robin Wagg, Lolai O'Dwyer, Andrew Ryder-Hockey, Anna Horrocks, Kim Jobst, Mark Hooper and Angela Rennells.

I would like to thank my mother and stepfather for their willingness to talk about anything and their belief in me; my father for his discerning mind and unconditional support; my brother,

Rupert, for being my rock and my friend, and for enduring years of totally conditional love from a bossy, older sister; and I must pay tribute to Grizzle, my cat, whose contributions on the word-processor have sadly had to be excluded.

Beyond which, my special thanks go to the Benfield family – Andrew, Lucy and Sarah.

Contents

Introduction

… for death is the destiny of everyone;
the living should take this to heart.

Ecclesiastes 7.2

At the age of twenty-eight, I had my first close encounter with death. It wasn't my own. It was the death of a woman in her sixties, whom I had known for a year. Although I had thought a lot about death, and had experienced my fair share of grief, I had been quietly dreading the first real confrontation with it. I was frightened by the prospect. I think I almost believed death was something that happened to other people and somehow I was going to get away with it. Furthermore, in a world which values survival and material gain above all, death must surely be the ultimate failure: the last laugh of a God who never cared in the first place.

I have since asked myself why we struggle to make room for death in our lives. We're not very good at dealing with death in the West. We would rather not talk about it; it's embarrassing and tactless. If we admit we think about it, we must surely be a little morbid. There are even some people who believe that the less they think about it, the longer they will live. That is all very strange considering the one and only certainty in our lives is that one day we will die. We will stop breathing, our bodies will return to dust and we won't be here any more. What is the fear that prevents us from taking the reality of death into our hearts? Should we listen to this fear or seek to go beyond it, in the hope that the face of death will change as we peer more closely into it?

My own experience convinced me that, whilst fear of death is only natural, it is not a good enough reason to shy away from it. And that the more it can be discussed, the more openly the feelings shared, then the more we can begin to 're-naturalize' death. If death becomes an integral part of our lives, it promises not just to leave us better prepared for our own dying and that of others, but also strengthens us in our ability to live brave and conscious lives. Lives where relationships are not crippled by the desire to avoid the pain of letting go and separation – processes which might give new life to an old relationship; where mid-life crises, and all other times when the soul screams for change, are welcome and become manageable. The secret revealed to us by a closer participation with death is that we acquire the power to transform and take greater control of our lives.

It was through Ann that I was introduced to the experience of death. I met her in May 1994, when she came to see me for the first time as a 'patient' at the Wantage Natural Health Centre. I was working one evening a week as a spiritual healer, and I think I was probably her last resort. She was sixty-three and had struggled with breast cancer for seven years. Radiotherapy had resulted in paralysis of her right arm; chemotherapy had kept her alive but had taken its toll. She wore a wig, her complexion was grey and her breathing laboured. Her body was too weak to support the latest round of chemotherapy and she'd been sent home – with two weeks to live.

I remember my own fears all too clearly, feeling hopelessly ill-prepared to be of help to someone so close to death. I had my beliefs, deep beliefs, and in my heart I knew God's love and compassion. I knew the peace that so often descended on people during a healing session. But faced with the reality of someone dying, I really didn't know if I was the right person. How could faith – hers and mine – touch the physical process of death? Could it make a difference to the quality of Ann's death?

The experience of the first healing session was unlike any I had

had before. When I put my hands on Ann, I had the sensation that her spirit, the 'real' Ann, was standing about two feet away from her body. And that her body was a shell – and a very sick shell. I felt so much compassion for her body; how hard it had tried to support her, how tired it was, how much pain it had endured. With Ann in it. I understood why she wanted perhaps to leave all that behind. And certainly the person standing beside her own body was anything but sick; she emanated a shining vitality. Freedom.

She left and I wondered if I would see her again. To my great surprise, she almost bounced in the following week, telling me she felt 'thirty per cent better': cheerful, optimistic, with renewed energy and a determination to stay alive. She didn't expect a complete recovery, but she wanted another year at least.

Every week throughout the summer, she came to see me and we 'worked' together. Her colour came back, her breathing improved and she began to get out and enjoy herself, spending as much time as she could in her beloved garden. For many years she had grown flowers for drying and both she and her son, Andrew, were well known in the village for their dried flower arrangements. I have one in my kitchen.

It was her courage that touched me most. She had a lot of worries, which she began to share as we got to know each other. She didn't want to die. But always there was a quiet faith within her, a gentle acceptance of all that was happening to her. She never lost her sense of humour and took enormous delight in walking down the corridors of the hospital, striding into the check-up room and apologizing for being on her feet and not in a coffin. There was even one occasion which found its way into the local newspapers.

She had fallen one night as she stood up to go to bed. Unable to get up, she had called for her son. Andrew came rushing downstairs, but, perhaps a little dazed from sleep, passed out when he saw his mother on the floor, knocking his head on a glass bowl as he fell backwards. The thudding crash woke his wife, who came to see what was the matter. She saw Andrew, and then Ann, and promptly passed out herself.

Someone at some point, however, had managed to call an ambulance, which arrived to find the entire family had 'dropped like nine-pins'. On entering the house, the dog had escaped and come to join in the fuss. Ann's last words, as she was lifted to safety, were: 'My wig! Get the dog off my wig.'

For a few months, Ann's vitality was extraordinary. Then, as the nights began to draw in, her health began to deteriorate. The first sign was her breathing; she began to find the clinic stairs exhausting and I suggested that I come to visit her in her home instead. I think that was perhaps the moment we both realized that the nature of our journey together had to change.

It was time to prepare for death. I had no clear idea of what that would entail. I never knew what to expect when I saw her, and in the end I could only love her. I remember my thoughts at this time; I went through quite a dilemma about what my role should be. Did I maintain some degree of professional detachment or did I abandon my role and 'get my hands dirty'? Was it my own fear or a genuine uncertainty about what would be most helpful to Ann that was causing the confusion? In the end, I decided I would walk with her as far as I could, and as closely as I could, and simply trust that God would protect and help us both.

And so our relationship changed and grew into one of deep friendship. We would share a cup of tea and a piece of cake in front of the fire whenever I visited; sometimes she talked about her family. She found it difficult to talk about herself and her own feelings about her illness. Often I felt it would have been important, but I didn't want to intrude. More dilemmas. And yet, in the healing session itself, the great peace would always descend and I sensed that whatever was really happening to Ann in that loving silence, it was reaching her soul. She was taking it in and, in the privacy of her being, it was helping her approach death with dignity and courage.

Then, in April, she was taken into the local hospice with a clot on her lung. The last week of Ann's life was a time I will remember for the rest of my own. I wrote about it as I understood it at the time in my diary; it was just before Easter.

Monday, April 3rd

Hard day today. When I went to see Ann yesterday, she said to me, 'If I can just hang on until the end of the week, I'll be all right to pop off at the weekend.' I'm finding Ann's struggle – and therefore my own struggle with her impending death – difficult to digest. I felt sick this morning. It is fear. Of the unknown and of trying to cope with this and the work pressures, which are intense at the moment. An extremely challenging time. I couldn't go to the hospice today, I just couldn't. I *have* to take care of myself too, otherwise I'll be no good to anyone. I need God more than ever at this time – to help me realize that I'm not alone and therefore I don't need to be afraid.

Tuesday, April 4th

I feel like crying. Crying. The strain. There is considerable grief and tension in my brain and a lot to sort out. But I went to see Ann, and, oddly enough, I gain strength from being with her. She was really pissed off and fed up today – three enemas. It is strange, but although her body is functioning less and less of its own accord, I don't feel as if Ann is 'dying'. Not in the way we think of death in this society - as loss, as ebbing, as misery. She is always Ann. In fact she is more of herself somehow, as if dying is creating a transparency of her body that leaves her spirit shining more readily through. Death feels so *natural*, so much a part of life. I know all the wisdom teaches us this, but until you see it for yourself, it doesn't filter through. It remains as received wisdom and it needs to be integrated knowledge.

One thing I do notice and find hard is how people around me are disappearing into thin air. Not wanting to be near me, as I go through this. Of course it hurts and it made me angry when I first noticed it, but now I think I understand. They're afraid. The world is very afraid of death so they try to avoid it. Which means me at the moment!

Wednesday, April 5th

Ann is so tired. So tired now – she's coming to terms with dying and it won't be long now. My dear, dear friend. How I love her. She's calm and comfortable enough; so tired she can hardly speak or even open her eyes. The effort is too much. She feels so precious to me, and when I left her tonight, I knew I'd left her in God's hands. He tends her constantly now. Helping her prepare for her onward journey, which could be any moment.

The healing was indescribably beautiful tonight. I'm *sure* someone was there. I could feel him, or a presence at least that was golden in colour. And warm, and so gentle. All around. And the closeness between Ann and myself was tangible. She seemed so breathtakingly beautiful to me. So beautiful. At the end, I had to tell her I loved her – I knew if I never said it that I would regret it, although I've often wanted to before. She glowed! And told me she loved me too.

Thursday, April 6th

I felt heavy and grief-laden this morning and so I sat outside Woodstock church and shed a tear or two. I tend to wake up feeling like this – tired before I even start the day, wondering how I'll get through and how Ann will be. Just taking where possible each moment as it comes. Today she was brighter, but a little confused at times. I'm not quite sure what she's saying most of the time but then suddenly she'll be incredibly lucid too. She talks to herself, or to someone, when I give her healing. Maybe she's slipping in and out now – of this world and the next. When I asked her if she was afraid, she said 'No, I'm not afraid'.

And I'm not afraid any more. I seem to be moving into a new stage of acceptance too. More detached. I'm conscious so much of others. This process is so alien and frightening to most people that they can't bear to look or hear – and rather than force it on them, I'm learning to keep quiet and do it alone – with Jesus. Then I don't frighten people. They don't get close either, which makes me sad and lonely, but I'm too much in it to stand back and help them at the moment. But if I let go of my expectations of friends, and family, then they're free to be themselves and to give what they can. And if I don't block *everything* just because I feel hurt and disappointed, then at least I receive a little in the way of human contact.

Saturday, April 8th

I didn't go to the hospice yesterday. And Ann died today. Part of me wishes I had, but the truth is I really needed a day's rest. My consolation is that I know – and Ann knew – that she's been in my heart constantly this last week.

I had planned to go to see her this afternoon, and so this morning I wandered into the church, walked up to the altar and stood for a while, thinking of Ann. Then I found myself saying 'When she asks for you, Lord, please be there for her', knowing that there was somehow nothing left for me to do and that the very last step was entirely her own. It was 11.45 a.m.

When Andrew phoned me after lunch to say she'd died, he told me it had been quick and peaceful. Somewhere between 11.40 and 11.45 a.m. She'd been sitting up happily in bed, placing a bet on the Grand National. I feel so overwhelmed with emotion – joy, gratitude, awe. I feel so *proud* of her. She did it! She really did it – just the way she wanted. Completely in tune with herself – bang on time. And she really did 'pop off'! Truly amazing. Dear Ann … my friend.

After Ann died, I felt bereft and drained for a while. I missed her, but I was surprised how quickly the hardness of the grief softened. I began to realize how lucky I was to have had that time with her, and to know there was nothing between us that was left unsaid or undone. It helped me take death 'to heart', and I truly believe that if we can all begin to do that, in our own way, it will make a difference. A difference to the daily, the hourly quality of our lives and our relationships. A difference that means when we do finally get to the end, if we're lucky enough to be conscious, we can look back at our lives and feel no regrets.

If we know that we loved as best we could, that we faced difficulties head on and moved through them, we can leave this world just a little better for having been incarnated into it. It has made me believe that the real tragedy of death is to realize we didn't really *live* during our allotted time; we didn't commit ourselves soon enough to an intimate relationship with ourselves and with others. And perhaps the fear we are so blinded by is the fear of taking full responsibility for our life.

As time passed, I began to want to talk about what had happened and why it is important for us to drag death from under the carpet and put it firmly back in front of the fire, where it belongs. I wanted to find out what other people had experienced and how they thought and felt. I wanted those people who have developed an intimate relationship with death to impart some of their wisdom and knowledge.

What follows in the rest of this book is a collection of personal interviews with a handful of such people. They have been chosen for their honesty and openness and because each person has something unique to contribute in the journey towards a greater understanding of death.

ANNA HOWARD
Woodstock
May 1996

I

Barbara and David Huelin

In 1989, the Huelins started to prepare for their deaths and funerals. Six years on, their hand-made coffins await them in the shed at the bottom of the garden, the family is fully briefed on its role as coffin-bearers, and plots have been booked in the local cemetery.

David Huelin is now eighty-one. Graduating from Oxford University in 1936, he spent the next fourteen years in Argentina, working first on the Argentine railways and then as Deputy Editor of a business magazine. On returning to England, he worked in the economic research department of the Bank of England and South America until he retired in 1974.

Barbara Huelin was born in 1926. She married her first husband at the age of twenty-one and went to live in Argentina. When the marriage broke down in 1948, she returned to England with her son. She and David married in 1952 and had twin daughters four years later. When David retired, they moved to Oxford to live in a house on the Oxford Canal; with the purchase of an elegant mahogany cruiser, they have together navigated virtually the whole of the inland waterways system.

DAVID:

'Death will come as a mild surprise; a momentary shudder in a darkened room.' That is really how I now feel about death. I think our story began around the time when we had to attend several funerals and we took a great dislike to the impersonal way in which they were handled by undertakers: the coffin arrived in a shiny hearse and was taken out by six men in black suits, carried into the crematorium, where it was put on a trolley, slid into the recess behind the curtains – and it was all over. Impersonal, detached, mechanical and anonymous. So we thought, when it came to our turn, we could do better than that. We were very keen that the family should be involved. We didn't want any men in black suits and we didn't want any undertakers ...

BARBARA:

And we didn't want a shiny coffin. Don't like that sort of thing, with its brass plates and satin lining.

DAVID:

So we thought about it for a time and decided that this was something we should organize for ourselves, the way we wanted it. Barbara went round Oxford, trying to find someone who would sell her a plain coffin ...

BARBARA:

Yes, I went round on my bicycle and called on four or five funeral directors. At first, they thought I had come because some dear one had popped off and I needed to organize the funeral. No, no, I said. It's not that. I just want to buy a coffin. Oh... They completely changed their attitude and told me they didn't do anything like that. They looked me up and down and said, 'Oh, there are plenty of years left in you anyway,' and, 'You wouldn't want to buy one now, even if you could, because of warpage.' 'I beg your pardon?', I said. 'Oh, yes. Warpage. You won't be able to get the lid on properly perhaps.'

I'd also seen an article in the *Guardian* about a bloke up in

Leicestershire who had a hardware shop; there was a photograph of him standing outside this old-fashioned shop – with two or three coffins beside him. So I rang him up straightaway and asked if I could buy two. He told me what measurements to take. Now, this is important because of course men and women are a different shape, aren't they?

DAVID:

You see, first of all there is the question of size. Barbara is quite a tall woman, so she needed something substantial. And also women tend to be wider at the hips than at the shoulders and men the other way round. If you want to get the coffin, as it were, *fitting*, you've got to get your measurements rather precise.

BARBARA:

Anyway, what happened was that when I rang the Leicester bloke after six months, he said he was sorry to tell me that his supply had dried up. Very odd. Well, it seems there was a sort of mafia involved in the funeral business and it was an absolute closed shop. The manufacturer of these cheap coffins had probably been rapped over the knuckles by the funeral directors for selling them to the public rather than to the trade.

We did not manage to buy a coffin. So, I said to David, who is a tolerable carpenter, 'Well, you must make them, and you'd better get cracking because you're seventy-six and you might die, so get started now.'

DAVID:

What you need for a coffin is wood that is rigid, but not too heavy. So I opted for blockboard. We bought three sheets and I cut out two coffins on the lawn with an electric saw. An awful lot of noise. But we warned the neighbours we would be making our coffins. One has to start with some sort of drawing. I took Barbara's measurements. I stood her up against the wall, traced her outline and then measured the dimensions. I drew that out on the blockboard and cut it up; then I assembled the bits in my workshop. But I made a mistake in choosing three-quarter-inch blockboard, when half-inch would have done just as well. So the coffins are a little bit heavier than they need to be.

So, having made our coffins, we needed to think about the day when we were going to have to use them. We asked the family how they felt about acting as bearers. They all said yes and we got together two teams of six – the First Six and the Second Six – members of the family and friends who are willing to come and do their stuff at a moment's notice. Of course, it's unlikely we'll both go together.

BARBARA:
Unfortunately. It would be rather nice to go together.

DAVID:
Do you think so? It would be rather a lot of bother for other people.

BARBARA:
No, it's much less bother if we die together. Much less bother … but David has left out the part of the story when we decided to be buried rather than cremated. Before we entered into all this, we always intended to be cremated; and so I suggested we go and look at the crematorium, because I wasn't at all sure that if we were cremated, we would get the right ashes. I'm not into having somebody else's.

We have a great friend called Ingrid who volunteered to drive us up to the crematorium. I had arranged an interview with the manager. He was thoroughly shaken by our questioning but when I brought up the business of the ashes, he made it quite clear that one would get the right ashes, which the crematorium will send by courier to the 'Bereaved'.

DAVID:
But it was in fact on that occasion that we really took a scunner at cremation, didn't we?

BARBARA:
Yes, it was a lovely day and when we'd finished our talk with the Manager we went out into the Garden of Remembrance, up onto the hill, and we looked up at the sky ... and what did we see?

DAVID:
As we went up the hill, we got more or less level with the top of the chimney of the crematorium and we saw hot gas coming out of it, blurring the view behind. We felt that the whole thing was a bit of a pollutant. In no small way, because the volume of hot gas coming out of that chimney was enormous. It wasn't smoke, I will say that – but it smelt. Moreover, the question of what to do with the ashes seemed rather tedious. You can't collect the ashes the same day because they're hot. The crematorium packs them up when they're cool and puts them into a plastic urn, which you can have on your mantlepiece if you like. I presume it's marked 'Not suitable for hot ashes'.

We decided then that cremation was not for us and we'd rather be put in the ground.

BARBARA:
We rang up the Oxford City Cemetery at Wolvercote and asked for an appointment. They turned out to be delightful people.

DAVID:

Hugh Dalton and Janet Simmonds. They are so nice and so helpful – and kind.

BARBARA:

You book your plot. We bought ours there and then: £125 for a double-decker. I believe you can pay thousands of pounds in some of the big London cemeteries. We chose our spot very carefully. First of all we were taken to an area which we felt was rather too close to the ring road. Ingrid thought the noise might keep us awake. Then we were taken round to an area that backs onto a wide open space, quite near where the gravediggers keep all their tools in a shed. And now some good friends have decided to have a plot near ours.

So, you see, when one of us dies, the other one isn't going to have horrible feelings of isolation, things happening around them that they don't know anything about, people around them that they don't know.

And the wonderful thing about burials at Wolvercote is that there are no strict rules about what you can and can't do. They had one funeral recently, for example, for an old boy who had led a local jazz band. And the band came along and played. It was a real celebration.

We must also talk about the question of help from an undertaker. We have been made aware that there are certain things that we are going to find quite difficult to do physically. One is if you die in an awkward place. I think of David passing out daintily in his bed one night, but he could crash down the stairs, or fall under a bus. You know, there are all sorts of not so dainty ways of popping off and they have to be taken into consideration. So we may well require the assistance of an undertaker for the physical moving of the body – and bodies are heavy – and the laying out, which of course in the old days was done by the district nurse and a member of the family. We wish our bodies to be kept in this house until the burial.

Another thing is that for some years we had children living in far-flung parts of the world. So if we had died during a hot summer and the burial had had to be delayed so that all the family could be present, maybe we should have had to consider embalming. So I had to find a funeral director who would do something they wouldn't have considered four or five years ago, and that is to give a partial service. I did find one and he got the message of what we wanted and agreed to it.

I wanted it all in writing – it's easy to forget that people at the time of a funeral are usually much too shocked and upset to ask for an estimate. But because we were quite fit at the time, we could ask him exactly what it was going to cost and get the costs broken down and agreed.

DAVID:

There was something here we hadn't given any thought to. What if we were to die in hospital or in a road accident? You end up in a mortuary and apparently it's not very easy for private people to retrieve bodies from these mortuaries. There is a sort of mafioso arrangement between the morticians and the undertakers. Our part-time undertaker agreed to tackle that job, if the need arose. He would bring the body to the house and put it in the coffin.

I tell you what else we have discovered over the years that we've been thinking about it seriously: conversation on the subject of death, disposal of dead bodies, burial, etc. becomes much easier once you start talking. And the effect of our discussing it with anyone who is interested has been to liberate the subject from the taboos that have traditionally hedged it in. The effect is to go back to the attitudes of the earlier centuries, when burials were done by the family, and the black-coated undertakers hadn't been invented. We coined a phrase, which is in fact now used by the Natural

Death Centre in London, namely that not talking about death doesn't keep it away; likewise, talking about it doesn't bring it any nearer. So why not talk about it and get rid of the taboo? So you can say, 'Death, where is thy sting?'

You ask whether that has made any difference to how we actually feel about our own deaths. I don't know. I think I've always been aware that it was something that was going to happen. It hasn't happened yet; it'll happen next year, or tomorrow. I don't mind. Possibly we have both got to the point where we see much more clearly how our funerals should be done by the family, without the intervention of officialdom or commerce and we have in fact gone into it in some detail. We're now so familiar with the subject that it's part of our conversation at any time and I think it's no exaggeration to say that we have shown other people how easy it is to talk about death and free the subject, let air into it. And since we're all going to die anyhow, why not face it and extract the poetry out of it, if you like.

BARBARA:

It hasn't changed anything. We just plod on, as always. I think a very important thing is that, after the first one dies, the survivor will have the great comfort of knowing that we did all this together and I can't help thinking that it will assist in the grieving. Because for years it's something that has been part of our everyday life; each time we go down to the shed, our coffins are there to remind us.

DAVID:

Obviously for the person who dies, death is not important. It's just the end of life. But for the survivors, it is important – and it's *very* important – that they should have well-prepared minds and know how to learn from the grieving process. The process should not be checked or blocked; people should be allowed to grieve and feel sad that they've lost the old boy, or the old girl.

BARBARA:

I think we also look on it as a celebration. That the life that is ended is to be celebrated.

DAVID:

It's a bit like the end of the opera, when the singers take a bow and then retire – and that's death. I hope people will applaud, as my curtain falls. I think there's a close parallel.

As far as life after death is concerned, well, I have no religious belief whatsoever. Absolutely none. For me, death is the cessation of life and that's it. The candle is out. I am a complete materialist and death doesn't worry me in the least. Every night when I go to bed, I wonder if I shall wake up in the morning. It doesn't bother me if I don't; in fact if I don't, I shan't worry, shall I?

BARBARA:

But you're going to be buried by a bishop! Originally our clergy-man son was going to conduct our burial services – and he does it beautifully – but now he says he would prefer to bear the coffins because he would be too emotionally moved to conduct a service. He has a close friend who is a retired bishop and who has said he will come and bury us.

And on the subject of religion, David and I differ. You see, I'm steeped in the Anglican background. I'm not a churchgoer, but during my childhood I could recite everything, and still today, if I go to Sung Eucharist, everything comes flying out. I adore the singing, I love the music … so I've prepared a great service for my funeral. With all my favourite hymns with all the tunes carefully marked. They've got to be the right tunes, otherwise I shall be banging my fists on the lid of the coffin.

DAVID:

Whereas I would just like somebody to read a few paragraphs from the *Essays* of Francis Bacon. I greatly admire these essays; they're full of wisdom, beautifully expressed. Let me give you an example:

> Men fear Death as Children fear to go in the Dark. And as that Natural Fear in Children is encreased with Tales, so is the other ...
>
> But above all, believe it, the sweetest Canticle is *Nunc Dimittis.*
>
> Francis Bacon, *Essays II*

And then there's the part of another essay that speaks about friendship:

> A principal Fruit of Friendship is the Ease and Discharge of the Fullness and Swellings of the Heart which Passions of all kinds do cause and induce. We know Diseases of Stoppings and Suffocations are the most dangerous in the Body; and it is not much otherwise in the Mind ... No Receipt openeth the Heart but a true Friend, to whom you may impart Griefs, Joys, Fears, Hopes, Suspicions, Counsels, and whatsoever liveth upon the Heart to oppress it, in a kind of civil Shrift or Confession.
>
> Francis Bacon, *Essays XXVII*

A funeral should be as individual as that person was in life. The quotations of Bacon, which I shall arrange to be read, are simply my way of saying 'Here I go' and this is my message as I leave.

Of course, we have enjoyed our children and grandchildren very much, but when we die we shall not be there to see them and we shall not remember. There is a sort of in-built kink in the human mind that assumes we shall be conscious of something after we're dead, and I suppose this instinct is the basis of Christian and other teaching. I don't think there is any life hereafter, and that's my firm belief. But the human mind seems to be imprinted with this belief and it's very difficult to get rid of. In our conversation, there has been this implicit assumption that there is some sort of life after death.

BARBARA:

Well, maybe there is! You're so categorical about it; I'm beginning to wonder.

DAVID:

Well, I have never experienced any indication of anything to the contrary. I have no evidence, no knowledge, no experience suggesting there is any life after death. Therefore I conclude there isn't. You ask how that affected me when my parents died. Well, my father died at home; my mother rang up very early one morning and said she thought he'd died and could I come. I went and, sure enough, he had.

BARBARA:

And what did you feel?

DAVID:

Certainly I was distressed. I was concerned about losing my father, but more than that, I was worried about how my mother was going to be. She was a pretty tough character and she took it very well, but I realize now I could have done more to make the funeral interesting and significant.

Of course not believing in an afterlife does make it more difficult when someone is grieving. It's a sort of instinctive comfort to believe the dead one is not dead. But I have never used that argument.

BARBARA:

We're at the age now when we often have to write letters to bereaved people and I think one has to be completely honest and straightforward. It's hypocritical to talk about an afterlife, if you don't believe in it. I'm not as categorical as David though – there is room for manœuvre!

2

Sir Isaiah Berlin

Sir Isaiah Berlin was born in the Baltic city of Riga in 1909. In 1915 the family moved to Petrograd; they lived through both Russian Revolutions before moving to England in 1919.

Sir Isaiah was educated at St Paul's School and Corpus Christi College, Oxford. He became Fellow of both All Souls College and New College, Chichele Professor of Social and Political Theory, and the first President of Wolfson College.

During the Second World War he was assigned to New York and transferred in 1942 to the Foreign Office where he served in the British Embassy in Washington until 1945, and then briefly in Moscow.

Philosopher, historian of ideas, proponent of liberal thinking and renowned conversationalist, Sir Isaiah is one of this century's most influential men.

We are all aware of the fact that we are going to die. We know that the world will carry on after us; if we have people who are close to us, we are worried about their fate.

I do not believe in a world after death. I see no reason for believing in one. I'd quite like it if it existed. I'm not against it. I'd rather like to think that there is a world after death and that we shall all meet in it people we love. But I don't believe it, because I see absolutely no evidence of it, and no reason for believing in it. It is just a comforting idea for people who can't face the possibility or probability of total extinction.

Supposing I did believe in another life, I dare say I might have been self-interested enough to try to be virtuous in order to earn my place in Paradise; or, again, I could cynically decide this wasn't worth doing, and decide that in any case I could not avoid being sent to hell. Or maybe to purgatory, where I would remain for a long time until allowed to go to one place or the other. But I don't believe in any of this. So it doesn't affect me in any way.

Virtue ought to be its own reward. We all do things because they are what they are and not because we believe we're going to be rewarded or punished. Of course, if there are rewards and punishments, people are affected – they're affected by the anticipation of one or the other, but I'm not because I don't believe in them. If I do anything, there may be consequences in my life, or even in this world after my death, but not in some other world.

One's life is governed by a morality. We all think that some things are good, some things are bad, some right, some wrong. One's morality tends to govern one's choice.

How did I acquire the values by which I live? I think I am like most people, partly the product of my culture in which I grew up, which probably encapsulates its own values. I do not propose to rebel against it, but then I'm not very rebellious by nature. There are people who reject the values they've been taught, or the culture to which they belong and go against it. I fully understand their motives, and in some cases respect and admire them, but I'm not temperamentally very disposed to that.

We didn't talk about death at home. I do not recall my parents ever talking about it. We talked about the death of individuals, but not about death *per se*. I think in fact they may have believed in a future life. I think my father hoped that there was a future life. In fact, when he was dying, he asked me if I thought there was going to be life after death. I said that yes, I did. That was a lie. A lie, which I uttered because he obviously wanted it to be so and hoped we'd be able to meet again, and I didn't want to tell him what I saw as the bleak truth. So I did not tell the truth, and I don't in the least regret it. Since I believed that nothing would follow one's death, why should I cause a dying father pain? I wasn't there at the actual moment of his death, and I don't know whether he knew he was dying. He died of leukemia, but I don't think he had ever heard the word. I don't think he thought he was doomed. He felt weak and ill and may have thought he might be declining, but hoped to recover.

My father was brought up as a Jew; his parents had believed in an afterlife. Orthodox Jews believe in a future life. He wasn't Orthodox himself, but I'm sure his family believed it, and towards the end of his life some kind of memory of what he used to believe in may have come back to him. I'm sure he didn't want to perish utterly. I am a Jew, but not a true believer. I was brought up in a very free, rather relaxed fashion, and so, although I deviated from orthodoxy, it wasn't a question of active rebellion.

About the idea of a blessed, or perfect life. It is clear to me that you can't have everything, because some values collide. The idea that there is some world in which there is perfect justice, perfect love, perfect truth, perfect happiness, is not valid. Some of these things are simply not compatible with others and that is true of our life here. One has to choose. In choosing one value, one thing or another, sometimes you may lose something else which you value. And that is always painful. That's what choice entails. Therefore, the idea that somewhere beyond there is a world in which all these values are compatible with each other, will form a harmony, doesn't make sense in any conceptual scheme that I know. If it is true, it doesn't refer to situations that I can conceive of.

Let me add this: if I was asked whether I would mind living for ever – most people say that they would not – I think I would not mind living for ever, always provided that whatever powers there be could guarantee the following: if I could retain one hand, one arm, one leg, one ear, one nostril, a sense of smell, taste, touch, some mental power, and did not have to suffer great pain – if I was guaranteed all that, and believed in the guarantee, I wouldn't mind living on and on. I'm by nature an observer, not a man of action. I am filled with curiosity and long to know, what next?

There are things I don't understand because they don't mean anything to me. I don't know what a spirit without a body would be like. People believed in an immaterial soul in the eighteenth century, as for thousands of years before. Some people tried to watch the dying, to see the soul escaping through the mouth or the nose; trying to watch very carefully in case they could 'catch' it as it escaped.

I've never seen someone at the moment of death. My father died in hospital; the doctors said he would go on living, and then I was rung up and told he was dead. My mother lived to a great age, and, again, I asked the doctor if I ought to be in London with her, might she soon die? No, I was told, she'll live at least another year. She died that night.

So I wasn't present when either of them died. I saw my dead father in his bed, when I had to go to the hospital to arrange for the death certificate. I had grown up with him, he was a very nice man, he was very fond of me, he didn't interfere with my life, we always got on very well with each other, I liked his company, he liked mine – and he was gone. I was very, very fond of him, devoted to him. And terribly sorry I'd see him no more.

About fear of death. The Greek philosopher Epicurus said something which I accept: 'Why are you afraid of death? Where you are, death is no. Where death is, you are not. What is it that you fear?'

Death is not an event in life, not something which will happen to one. One is not aware of it. One may be aware of dying, of a painful process of becoming weaker and weaker and, perhaps, of suffocating, whatever it may be. But one is not aware of the actual moment of death. Therefore, if death is what one is afraid of, it won't happen, it won't be part of one's conscious experience.

I, too, am afraid of dying. But only if it's painful. Like everyone else, I would like to die in my sleep. Or be knocked down by a car and not feel it. I'd like the lights put out at once. I don't want to get more and more tired or have a long painful illness. I wouldn't like that a bit. If I was very ill and I knew I was dying, I would like euthanasia. I'm in favour of it. I don't know why people are left to suffer when it's quite clear that they can't go on living. People say God gave us life and it is not ours to dispose of. If you believe that, this argument follows. I don't believe it and therefore I think it is cruel not to terminate people's lives if the alternative is a long period of useless, inevitable suffering.

I think about death more now that I am so old. But only in the sense of wondering when I'm going to die. I've lived so long and I'm astonished I'm still alive. I really find it very surprising. I never thought I'd live to this age. When I was young, I'd never met anyone who was eighty – I'm eighty-six! The first time I met people of eighty was in All Souls College in Oxford in the 1930s. There were two old men there. They were ancient monuments! Most people didn't talk to them, they seemed remote from daily life. Old men to me were academics of sixty-five, at most sixty-seven, for example Gilbert Murray, and H. A. L. Fisher, Warden of New College, who had been a Cabinet Minister under Lloyd George. Eighty-six is very old. Too old, some people would say. But I feel perfectly well; I've just had a pacemaker and feel better as a result. I don't know when I shall die, but I'm astonished not to be dead already. Astonished and delighted! When I go to bed at night now, I say to myself that I really ought to be very pleased if I wake next morning. It is a thought, but it doesn't linger with me.

I wouldn't like to be told when I am going to die. That would feel like a pressure upon me, of a disagreeable kind. I live from moment to moment. Every day is a day. I don't want to say 'Three more years, and whatever you can do, you've got to do within that'.

I don't want to know I'm due to die – it's the last thing I want to know.

I used to dwell on the past a great deal, when I was younger. Before the war, for example, I thought about the past much more than I ever thought about anything else. For some reason, since the war – maybe it was after marriage – I haven't thought about it in the same way. I think about the past, because I remember it. I remember it because a man is writing my biography and he keeps asking me questions. So I try to remember. But on the whole, I don't dwell on the past. Nor on the future. I think about the present. And not much about that – I just go on living. Living, acting, seeing, talking, hearing, reading. I'm not very self-conscious. Nor have I ever been ambitious; I have never aimed at something in the future. I'm simply telling you what I'm like and there are probably millions like me.

The people I meet aren't obsessed with death, as far as I know – at least, they don't talk to me about it. Particularly my contemporaries. There are some people of my own age who are still alive: Stephen Spender, who died the other day, was my exact contemporary. I knew him as an undergraduate in Oxford. I don't think he brooded about death – well, he must have done because he was ill towards the end of his life and he must have had thoughts about it. In fact, one of his doctors was cruel enough to tell him that he didn't think he'd live very long. But he didn't talk to me about that. We behaved as if everything was perfectly normal, as if we would live for ever.

W. H. Auden must have thought about death, because he became a Christian. He could be very amusing at times on the subject. 'I will tell you', he said, 'what I think purgatory is like' (Catholics believe in Purgatory, but he believed in it too because he was basically Anglo-Catholic). 'It is like this: you are locked up in a room with somebody whom you have utterly despised all your life. Not just hated, that would be easier, but despised, couldn't bear to be with, held in the deepest contempt. When you've learnt no longer to despise him or her, and begin to love this person, then you are let out.'

I remember that Bertrand Russell, who was of course an atheist, when someone asked him, 'Mr Russell, supposing after you die, you find there is another world and you meet God – what will you say to him?' Russell said, 'I would say – well, why on earth didn't you give better evidence of your existence?'

I am moved by religious feeling. If I read religious poetry or prose, when I am in churches, synagogues, mosques, I am moved because I understand religious emotion. I am moved by prayer, or sacred music, by the expression of spiritual experience. But theology I do not begin truly to understand.

You ask how relevant the Holocaust is for me in all this. Well, I learnt about it much later than a lot of people, I'm ashamed to say. I was in Washington during the war, at the British Embassy. Nobody there talked about it; there were scarcely any Jews apart from me. I assumed, from 1940, that something dreadful was being done to Jews under the Nazis, but not in particular what. I assumed they were being killed or tortured, done away with in every way. But no news of the gas chambers leaked out publicly, or, if it did, it never got to me. There probably was something about mass extermination in the newspapers in about 1943. But I never saw it. The first time I ever knew of it was in early 1945. Well, of course I experienced the same sense of horror as most decent people, and the fact they were Jews brought it closer. I felt stupified by it – six million dead? one million? one hundred thousand? Mass murder is mass murder. The numerical part doesn't make a difference. I just felt this was the greatest single crime ever committed by anybody in known Western history. I still think so – but Stalin's acts come very close or are perhaps even more terrible. This is the most terrible century in Western history. I think the first time people were really aware of the German horrors was when the first photographs appeared out of Buchenwald and Belsen. This wave of horror went over the entire world. That was in 1945. My grand-parents were murdered – they came from the town of Riga, where I was born, on the Baltic. My grandmothers were dead, but my grandfather, his brother, their daughters, my mother's brother – all exterminated, quite early, in 1941. I didn't know this, but when I learnt of it, I was dreadfully shaken. I could not quite conceive of it; I could not imagine it.

I lack imagination. I lack capacity for macabre imagination; I'm not haunted and I don't brood. Things don't constantly crop up and drive me into a melancholy or neurotic state. I'm very unneurotic. I do remember a lot, and I enjoy remembering, but I'm not a victim of my memories. I am not aware of repressing anything – still, a competent interrogator might turn something up. You don't believe that I need psychoanalysis? True. I wasn't married until quite late in life and I thought I would never marry, that nobody would wish to marry me. I assumed that I was not attractive to women. So I never approached them as others did, and that might be a little abnormal. But in the end, it all happened. Late in life. My wife is eighty and I'm eighty-six and we have lived together very happily for about forty years. We still do. I have known very little missing in my life – I feel at once slightly ashamed and yet happy about this. I've had a fuller and more contented life than I probably deserve.

3

Dadi Janki

The Brahma Kumaris World Spiritual University
was founded in Karachi, now part of Pakistan, in
1936, in recognition of the need for self-transforma-
tion in order to bring about lasting peace in the
world. Dadi Janki is a founder member of the organization and has spent the last sixty years of her life
dedicated to the spiritual service of others.

She was born in 1916 in Sind and joined the
original community of 300 at the age of twenty-
one. She nursed the seriously ill during the first
fourteen years of her spiritual apprenticeship, much
of her understanding coming from her own ill
health. She came to the West in 1974 and has spent
the last twenty-one years expanding the University's
work. There are now 3,000 centres in sixty-two
countries, offering courses in meditation and an
education in spiritual and moral values.

'The organization actually teaches individuals to
develop virtues and a quality of life. Human beings
have been stumbling in the name of religion for so
long, but through a recognition and understanding
of the true value of community, that stumbling can
finish.

Greed, fear and hopelessness have made homes
in people's hearts. What is needed is to let go of all
old things and for you to allow yourself to become
true and clean. We now have the opportunity to
change our attitude and perceptions. Time is calling
us, the world is calling us and if you listen, your
own inner voice is calling you.

But even if time is calling you, without self-realization you will not listen. Look at what time is saying; look at the present situation of the world. You have to think about your own future and the future of the world. Be willing to let go of the past and change. When we change, the world changes.'

My spiritual roots are Hindu and, like all religions, we have our own understanding of death and of what happens to the soul when it passes on. Everybody is afraid of death and it is because of that fear of death that people perform good actions. They make sure they do not perform wrong actions. There are many examples of people who are not very religious, but as they come closer to the point of death, they become more and more aware of their own lives and engage themselves in acts of charity. They will feed the poor, they will find themselves an image of God or of a deity, they will start to read scriptures or listen to holy songs, so that there is something positive going into their minds.

There is also the belief that people shouldn't suffer too much in their sickness, they should receive help at the time of death. People believe that the kind of life they have led will come before them at the point of death – there is a sort of life review. And so they engage themselves especially in positive and good things at that period. If good things come in front of them as they are dying, their face begins to smile, so that, even though they may be sick, they don't seem as if they are sick. And other people are amazed when they look on the radiant face of a sick person. All of this means that when the spirit leaves the body, it leaves the body with pleasure, in comfort. A person, a soul, who leaves the body in that way – sitting in God's remembrance – makes people very happy. They recognize that the soul is very fortunate to be leaving the body in the awareness of God.

It is often just before dying that a person will become aware of not wanting attachment, greed or any other negative quality. If they have made mistakes, done something wrong, or hurt people then they ask for forgiveness before they die. Whatever debts they have to settle, they will try to settle in time, to enable their soul to leave the body in peace.

Nowadays people write wills, but they only come into effect after the person has died and there are often so many complications and legalities, especially in the West. If you have something of value, it is better to give it before death.

When the soul leaves the body, it takes another body instantly. The wish is that the soul should take another body immediately; it shouldn't wander around without a home. When somebody dies unexpectedly, from an accident, murder or whatever, then it is always wished that an atmosphere is created around that soul to enable it to move on quickly. If that doesn't happen and the soul is pulled back to its previous home, an atmosphere of heaviness descends. The right preparations haven't been made and the soul has not been able to move onto its new destination. It is one of the laws of Nature; that if one connection is broken – which happens when the soul leaves the body – then it *should* immediately move on to the next life. It should immediately enter the womb of the next mother. If the connection from the previous life hasn't been broken, the new family cannot feel that sense of belonging to their new baby; they have a sense that the being that has come to them is not theirs. Only if the connection from the previous family is broken can there be an accurate connection with the new. It is important to remember that although there is always sadness when a soul leaves one body, there is always happiness when it enters another. This knowledge can help people let go of their loved ones.

It is a very subtle process. In fact, the soul determines from the quality of its actions in the previous life where it goes. It is the law of karma. The quality of my interaction with others will lead me to my next family. The soul will go wherever there is connection.

There are three types of human being. One variety is those who just don't make any preparations for death. They spend their life so engrossed in earthly and material things, things they call pleasure, that it is as if they are not even aware that death is ever going to come to them. They know that there is such a thing as death, but they don't prepare for their death. They're very careless.

A second variety is those who have an understanding of right and wrong; they know that they shouldn't perform actions that would make them suffer later on. They know that whilst they are alive, they should give happiness and pleasure to others; that they should share happiness and claim blessings from others.

The third variety consists of those who are always ready for death. They do not know when they are going to die, but they have prepared themselves so that they will be free from attachment to the body. They have forged such a close link with God that it is as if they are sitting in God's eyes when they leave the body. It is as if such people are totally beyond the cares of this world, that nothing can pull them down. It is as if when others look on these people, they are reminded of God.

There was a time when I was at the point of death. Everybody was expecting me to leave my body. This was about thirty years ago, and the founder of the organization, a man called Dada Lekhraj (Brahma Baba), sent a recorded message to me saying, 'When you die, nobody will need to remind you of God, but you will remind others of God.' And it is as if that has worked as a blessing for me; I always have the thought that when I die, I will die reminding others of God. I won't die with suffering; I will die with happiness. I know that when I leave the body, I will fly like an angel. It's not an idle fantasy. I have this feeling because I am creating a personality like that here and now – in my life.

In fact, there have been four or five occasions when I nearly died. Thirty years ago was the first time and at that time I remember thinking that if it was true that my body was too sick or too weak to carry on, then I didn't mind leaving. Everybody was asking me how I felt about dying and I remember saying: 'Okay. If it comes, it comes. But I prefer not to die at this moment in time, because I feel that I can do a lot of service for others.' I felt that I wanted to serve others now in this body, because if I were to become a little child again, what could I do as a child? I knew that I would be a good child, but I would do more service in this body. Just as I felt that I was going to leave my body, I felt as if I was having a conversation with God. I asked God how it was that Brahma Baba, who was so much older than me, was still able to do service and why it was that I was having to leave the body. I was fifty years old. I felt that if my life was a little longer, I could work more. I was sitting in meditation and felt that my body was absolutely gone, it wasn't capable of doing anything. It was as if it was dead. And then suddenly it was as if life returned and God gave me another life.

Between 1981 and 1983, again I was very unwell. I could hardly speak at that time. Doctors said to me then – and they still do now – that I worked my body as if it was a donkey. They told me that even a donkey needs to rest sometimes and I was working my body too hard. Obviously the body is like a vehicle, and as it gets older, or if it runs out of fuel, it starts to react. But even if my hands don't work, my legs don't work, that's fine. My mind can work. I can do certain things through my mind. I can do service through creating good vibrations. So for those three years, although my body wasn't well, it wasn't that my service was any less. It just meant that after the first meditation of the day, which is at 4 a.m., people would come to me in my room instead of me going to them.

It is the feeling of wanting to serve others that gives inner strength. I have forged a link with God and so I continue too to receive God's love. I never get tired of my sicknesses. I have experienced most types of sickness! When I was much younger, I used to fall ill regularly because I had tuberculosis. This was when the organization was just beginning, about sixty years ago, and I was a nurse for this community of 400 people. So I was playing both roles – being sick and looking after the sick! And I asked one of the people responsible for the organization why it was that I was always falling sick and she said 'Sickness comes to you so that you become experienced and so that you are able to sympathize with others who are sick; you will know the pain that they are going through too.' You learn compassion.

When I begin to serve others, then I forget my own sickness, and as I forget it, then my sickness also goes away.

I do sometimes have a pull to go up there – to leave my body and be with God. In fact, I have the feeling that I have gone. I remember one particular occasion, when I think I was gone for a few hours. I had the feeling that I was looking at my body lying on the bed; and the people walking past me felt that I wasn't there at all. I didn't know that I was 'dead'. I only knew what I was experiencing and that when I returned again, I remembered I hadn't been in my body.

When the soul leaves the body, the soul experiences total light. It is not something physical. It is the experience of light and of the power of God. The feeling at the time was as if God's power was pulling me towards him. Usually when people leave the body, they feel that there is darkness in front of them, but when a yogi, who's had that endeavour to experience a relationship with God, leaves the body, then there is light in front of them and they experience themselves to be very close to God. When a soul leaves a body, it is not possible to see with the physical eyes, but it is possible to know. To understand that the soul is gone. There is a sensation that light has left a body and the room is for a while filled with that light.

But now, even while I am in the body, I experience that. That coming and going is not difficult. It's like going from ground floor, to first floor, to second floor. It's as if light is going through different levels, from the level of talking, to movement and silence, then beyond that no movement even. Just silence. And this is my practice during the whole day. So I am here now to speak to you, but when I have finished, I will go away from here to another realm. Where there is first only movement, and then on to where there is only absolute stillness and silence. It is called 'dead silence'. For me, there is total joy in that silence. There is no sorrow.

And this is my service. I continue to live so that I can give that experience. When I was still working as a nurse in the institution, about five or six people died in my lap and I had the feeling that this was indeed the state in which souls should leave the body. And now, if anyone is sick, I am very happy to visit them in hospital. There is someone at the moment, an old man who is very ill in hospital. I went to see him about three days ago and as soon as he saw me, his face lit up. It was as if life returned … and it is the giving of those vibrations that helps people.

At the end of the day, however, it is not up to me whether I live or die. It is up to God. In 1991 again I was at that critical point. I was ready to go; I had wound up everything; even my passport had expired! I was in India at that time and had double pneumonia. On the night of December 31st, I felt myself passing on. But God sent me back. So now, since no one can remember the actual date of my birthday, we celebrate it on January 1st!

I made a slow recovery from that time and was much better by April. I thought that I wouldn't have to travel any more, that I could just stay in India, but I felt as if I had another message from God telling me to go back to the West. Because if I am there in the physical body, people can receive directly the light and power of God. And I am still travelling worldwide; last year I must have got on a plane at least a hundred times. I spend about three months of the year in India and the rest of the time abroad.

It is the power of meditation, the power of God's remembrance that gives me the strength for this service. People say I don't age and the only reason is because time isn't wasted. Every moment of my time is used in a proper way. But I do have the desire one day to stay with God.

There does come a point when the soul does not need to return to another body. There comes a point when the cycle of time spins, we all return home to our home of light. But then we have to come back down again in a different way, in a life of purity, of joy. A divine life. The life of a deity. And I would like that; to come back at that time. I am prepared for that and when I return in that way, I will be very beautiful. At that time, the body will be beautiful, the soul will be beautiful. At the moment, the soul is beautiful, but the body is not beautiful!

At the moment, the five elements that constitute our earth have also become degraded because the human spirit has become degraded. It is because of the degrading of the human spirit that it creates chaos in our lives, but when the spirit becomes pure and divine, then the elements will also become pure and they will be ready to serve us. It will be heaven on earth.

4

Dame Cicely Saunders,
OM, DBE, FRCP

Dame Cicely Saunders is the founder of the modern hospice movement. She trained initially as a nurse, and then as a medical almoner when she was invalided out of nursing. Although the emphasis in the 1940s was more practical, the role of an almoner was very similar to that of today's medical social worker. During this time she became a Christian and found great solace from her relationship with God; solace which grew into a sense of vocation and a desire to serve. In 1947 she fell in love with a dying man, an experience which fused within her three important things: the desire to relieve people's pain, the desire to serve God, and the desire to know love. Out of this was born the idea for the hospice movement. Cicely Saunders trained as a doctor and in 1965 the foundations of St Christopher's Hospice were finally laid. She is now Chairman of St Christopher's, Sydenham, a hospice committed to giving the best possible palliative care to the terminally ill, whether that be within the hospice or in the home.

> Death closes all; but something ere the end,
> Some work of noble note may yet be done.
> Alfred, Lord Tennyson: 'Ulysees'

The journey that eventually led to the foundation of St

Christopher's goes back a long way – before I met my first founding patient. It goes back to when I was a trainee social worker, having been invalided from nursing, when I chose to go to what was then the Royal Cancer Hospital, now the Royal Marsden. I wanted to look at the needs of people with cancer, including the far advanced.

When I started in my first ward as a medical social worker in July 1947, I met a Polish Jew aged forty, whose name was David, who had come from the Ghetto in Warsaw. I think he had left before the war in fact, because he certainly wasn't there in the uprising. He had an inoperable cancer of the rectum and had just had a colostomy, but he didn't know that this was the scene. He was a loner, having lost his family, and was living in digs just off the Tottenham Court Road, so I kept an eye on him in outpatients. I discovered that he was an agnostic Jew, a very lonely person working as a waiter.

When he collapsed in the following January of 1948, his landlady got onto me and I said that I would go and see him.

When I got there, his doctor had seen him and David was waiting for admission to the Archway Hospital in Highgate. There he was in his small room and when he asked me if he was going to die, I said yes, he was. This was news to him and he was glad to be told. For the next two months, I visited him I suppose about twenty-five times and we became very fond of each other. He was a very interesting person – very direct. He would always say he was just a simple chap, but in fact he really wasn't. His grandfather had been a Rabbi and he was a thinking man. We used to talk about somewhere that might have helped him more than the very busy surgical ward of the hospital he was in. I helped him to make his will with the solicitor and he said he wanted to leave me something – to be 'a window in your home'. After that, he said to me 'Can't you say something to comfort me?' and so I recited the twenty-third Psalm. He asked me to go on and so I said the Venite (Psalm

95), and then I said Psalm 121. By that time, I had really reached the end of the psalms I knew by heart, because of course having sung in choirs I knew quite a lot. So I asked him if I should read to him and he said 'No, I only want what is in your mind and in your heart.'

I was already by then a diligent and evangelical Christian and I used to go to prayer meetings regularly. After David died, I went to one of my meetings, where we started to sing 'How sweet the name of Jesus sounds', and I thought to myself 'but it didn't to him'. Suddenly I knew I was being told something, tapped on the shoulder as it were … 'He knows Me far better than you do already.'

Within that story are the three things which became very important bases to the Hospice and my commitment to helping people coming to the end of their lives: 'openness' – of the window to the world, to our patients and their families, openness among ourselves and, really, openness to the Beyond. Then there's 'mind': everything of science, of research, of understanding, of learning, that we can give people, together with the friendship of the heart. Mind and heart must go together. The third one is respect for the individual; David had made his own way, his own journey in the freedom of the spirit. So I am never to worry about people, never to worry that they won't find their own way.

When I saw David, I didn't think of death or of a dying person. It was just David, who was in need. The idea of my own mortality and all that, which people always talk about and often think about when faced with death, didn't particularly arise. It was much more simple; it seemed to be my place. To care for the dying.

However, I needed to test this sense of vocation and I made the decision to go to St Luke's Hospital in Bayswater, which had forty-eight beds for patients dying of cancer. I did seven years there as a volunteer, going on a Monday evening on the number 12 bus from St Thomas's – and because I was a trained nurse, they made me a

Sister for the evening. They were that short of staff! I used to sing to the patients, accompanying myself, which I didn't find particularly easy but I did have rather a sweet, soprano voice and they seemed to like it. But later Matron produced a lovely Salvation Army pianist who used to accompany us, so I had a very fine rendering of various things.

By the time I had done about three years there, I knew it really was my place, and I told the surgeon I was working for that I would have to go back and nurse the dying. I thought that I could perhaps get a job as a night sister at St Columbas. But he told me to go and read medicine: 'It's the doctors who desert the dying, and there's so much more to be learnt about pain. You'll only be frustrated if you don't do it properly, and nobody will listen to you.' He was absolutely right. My father was delighted, having wanted me to read medicine, and told me not to worry about money. Mr Barrett then did me a bit of a push to get me into St Thomas's Medical School, and I started from scratch at the age of thirty-three.

I didn't mind being an older student at all, because I always had this strong sense of knowing where I was going. I was going to do something about people like David – their pain, their symptom control, their need to be talking to somebody else about who they were, what had happened in their lives. There was David, dying at the age of forty, thinking that he had done nothing and there was no ripple on the pool to show he'd ever been.

So I plodded through my training and I got through well. I got Distinction in Surgery – no business to have done that; it was just because I knew how to take exams. I did my house-jobs and then got myself into St Joseph's to work among dying patients, to introduce the regular pain control which they had been doing at St Luke's. This was the regular giving of oral opiates – morphine in their case – and it was really like waving a wand over the house. I'm still in touch with the sister whose ward I started working in in

October 1958. She's written to me a few times and still remembers the difference in patients who went almost overnight from painful to pain-free, and how helplessly she had watched the pain people were in before I came on the scene. They were virtually untouched by medical advance and it was wonderful to be able to develop it there.

All through this time, I was very actively involved with Christianity. There was a thriving Christian Union at St Thomas's and I had a wonderful time there. People did think I was a bit eccentric, but I didn't mind. I remember when I was a houseman, I was visiting a friend at St Thomas's, carrying a bunch of freesias, and I met a former colleague, who said to me, 'If ever I see you coming to visit me with a bunch of flowers, I shall be very uneasy.'

After I qualified I wanted to carry on learning and got a Clinical Research Fellowship, via my father. He had run into the Head of the Department of Pharmacology at St Mary's, Paddington – they used to play tennis together in our garden – and Professor Stewart gave me a job at St Mary's. The condition was that I could get access to patients, and I got access at St Joseph's on condition they didn't have to pay me. So it all worked out.

It was whilst I was working at St Joseph's in this capacity that I became more aware of the nature of pain – that it wasn't only physical. There was one particular patient, a Mrs Hinson, who really encapsulated my understanding of pain when she said to me:

> Well, Doctor, it began in my back but now it seems as if all of me is wrong. I could have cried for all the pills and the injections, but I knew that I musn't. Nobody seemed to understand and it seemed as if the world was against me. My husband and son were marvellous, but they were having to stay off work and lose their money. And it's so wonderful to begin to feel safe again.

She had talked about the physical, the emotional, the social/ family, and the spiritual need for safety – which then gives the freedom to be yourself. As a result, I talked and lectured about total pain with those four elements. As far as the patient is concerned, it's actually a whole experience, but if you have a little checklist in your mind, it can help you understand. One may be more important than the other, of course, but they're all relevant.

Patients want their pain relieved. There are a few odd naturists who don't want any drugs, even though morphine is a good, natural drug, but most patients want relief from the physical pain. They certainly want relief from anxiety and depression and to bring the burden into manageable proportions; they want to be able to relate to their families. Because they're in crisis, they're moving fast. People always do in a crisis and they're concerned with some kind of resolution. As Pope John XXIII said, 'I've packed my bags, I can go with a tranquil heart any time.' Even if they don't think they are going anywhere, I think they do have a feeling of wanting to bring their lives together and know something of themselves before they lay it down.

I started lecturing in 1959 and also wrote a series of articles for the *Nursing Times*, which were published as a little booklet in 1960. I put down a lot of my ideas about the needs of patients there. My opening chapter was on euthanasia, and although I still don't agree with it, I wouldn't argue the way I did then any more. I argued then very much from the Christian point of view, talking about the sanctity of life. You need to work at the same level as the people you're arguing with and so I talk now about social pressures, the loneliness and problems of elderly people who feel they are burdens.

Everything I was doing was leading me nearer to founding the first hospice. Ever since my Damascus Road experience in 1945 I had been growing in my faith and I had developed a strong Bible background, but really it was the practical side that drew me. The Martha side and the Mary side were always about together, but basically I'm a Martha and not too much a Mary. Which means

I'm not really a contemplative type; I do have my time in the mornings but I start by reading Scripture. I've gone back to reading *Daily Light*, which I was reading when I was founding St Christopher's, and then I read part of the psalms for the day. I'm not a silent, emptying the mind and all the rest of it type – Sister Swallow is my mind.

I suppose it is the more personal experiences which have given me what I would call a right to speak. It was in the midst of working at St Joseph's and planning St Christopher's that I fell in love with another dying man – Antoni. He was Polish and had left Poland as a prisoner during the war. It has been said that in the face of death, love may flow from the heart of comforter and comforted alike, and that here above all a hidden nobility may find its true expression. Montaigne said, 'In the last scene between ourselves and death, there is no more pretence. We cannot but display such goodness and purity as lies at the bottom of our soul.' It is the fact that I fell in love with two people who were dying which shows that people are important right up until the last moment and that in the face of death, something new can happen.

I never feel, with anybody, 'Oh, you poor thing. You're dying.' People are just themselves and what I have always said is 'You matter because you are you. And you matter to the last moment of your life.' And that grew out of saying to Antoni, 'You matter because you are you.' It's important that people know they are special. When people come in here, they often say 'I'm a person again'.

Antoni fought to live until his daughter passed her exams and in fact that was the moment when she said to me 'My father has so much fallen in love with you, Doctor'. That started it off really and we had just three weeks left. Antoni was terribly important in that I was able to follow his journey along with him from 'I do not want to die, I do not want to die' to 'I only want what is right'. And we travelled our own paths in that same way. I was able to let go as he was able to do the same. I wasn't afraid of death – it was his release.

He was a deeply believing Christian, a devout Catholic, and I remember him looking at the crucifix on the wall in the next bay and saying 'I can see my Saviour' and I was able to say 'and he's mine too, and when you're gone, he'll be between us and that's where we'll meet'. After he died, I would have quite liked to die myself for a while, but I did gradually grow up into those words.

Certainly Antoni had kept himself alive for that one particular event, but it's very difficult to say exactly why some people live longer than others. A fighting spirit is seen as probably making people live longer. Research done by Stephen Greer, first at King's College Hospital and then at the Royal Marsden, shows that people with a fighting spirit live better and longer than those who are hopeless, helpless or who completely deny that there is anything happening.

It was three years after Antoni's death that I met Marian. I knew him for over thirty years, although we were only married for fifteen. His first wife was still alive in Poland when we met and then he couldn't get around to asking me, because he was afraid he might be marrying me for my money. Eventually he came and woke me up in the middle of the night and said, 'Will you marry me, as long as it's secret?'

We kept it secret for six weeks, then of course it got out and everybody was delighted. We had a blissful fifteen years together; he really was a bit of a wild artist, but he tamed at the end. He said some really wonderful things, which I wrote at the back of my diary and copied out after he died. 'We have found ourselves.' 'You enable me to be myself.' 'I'm happy now as I never was.'

Marian was very ill towards the end of his life, but I was able to keep him at home up until the last six weeks. His last weeks were spent here, in the Hospice. Wherever possible, we do try to care for the dying where they want to be. So if it's at home, we go to their home. But people often change their minds. Professor John Hinton carried out a survey, following seventy-seven patients from the moment they were referred for home care to the moment they died. Eighty or ninety per cent of their time was spent at home. All of them said at the beginning that they wanted to die at home; half of them said they wanted to come in to the hospice when it actually came to it.

You also have to remember the needs of the carer when someone is dying of a terminal illness. We have a respite care group of nurses who will go out and stay in the home for hours, which district nurses can't do. This gives the carer a break. In my own case, however, Marian just got too heavy and after one disastrous night I realized he had to go in. We had the weekend for Marian to come to terms with it, to say goodbye to his room. Quite honestly, the worst moment was when the steward asked how long he was staying this time and I had to say 'for good'.

Saying goodbye is very important for everyone concerned. We've had quite a lot of people who've had conflicting times in their married or family life but as they face death together, they find reconciliation or resolution. Ideally you want to be able to let the dying person go and you have to have a degree of satisfaction before you can let go. But if that doesn't happen, it's important that carers are not left feeling guilty.

Talking to children about the loss of a parent is, of course, another important area and is a particular concern of our Director of Social Work. You have to be honest. People don't want to be honest because they think that children will only be upset, but of course they are upset if they're isolated. Children are very basic; they're going to grieve and it's terrible for them if they're shut away from the family. They can choose to go to the funeral or not, but generally it's better if they do go. Age is largely irrelevant in this respect: even a four-year-old can take on board that Mummy isn't coming back. Teenagers in fact often find it more difficult, because they're busy trying to separate. They have to come back and say goodbye, and that can be hard. But children need to see that other members of the family can cry, because they learn that crying is what you do if you're sad and it's perfectly all right to do that. It harms, it doesn't help, a child if he or she doesn't see other people crying.

Always we are seeking to let each person die 'a good death' and that is of course different for everyone. The 'good death' may be 'I am very angry', and that is very hard for us, but if someone is angry and they don't resolve that anger, we just have to let them go angry. It doesn't happen very often, and the staff always find it very difficult when it does. But I'm quite sure they are met and that their anger is coped with on the other side. The majority of people find peace.

As far as what I believe happens to us after we die, well, we shall see. I think we see the light and fire of love and hopefully we go towards it, like the dwarf in one of C. S. Lewis's Aslan stories: it burns, but if you run away from it, it turns to darkness. There's a lovely passage in the Carlo Carretto book *The Spirit of St Francis of Assisi*, which refers to the door which is Christ that we all have to pass through. It is always fearful, like facing a great sea, but suddenly as the sea parts, there is this explosion of joy:

> Life and death were but two aspects of one and the same thing, as also sorrow and joy, light and darkness, cold and heat.
>
> It was as though the real were cut in half by a door.
>
> With good reason had Christ chosen the image: 'I am the door.'
>
> The door is the same on both sides.
>
> The earth, the visible, the tangible, time and space, are on this side; heaven, the invisible, the eternal, the infinite, are on the other side.
>
> But everything is one, congruent, logical and true.
>
> The door which is Christ simultaneously rules the here and the beyond with his love, crucified on this side, glorified on the other.
>
> To become immortal and enter the glory of the Risen Christ, everyone must pass through this door, and the One who opens

and closes it is the Lord. As Revelation says, 'If I open, no one closes.'

And creatures, through him, have two aspects: one crucified, here, and one glorious, beyond.

Nobody can escape this fact, and hence the death of each individual has a sorrowful aspect in the here-now and a glorious aspect in hope.

Our passing is always a fearsome ordeal, like looking at a boundless sea – and then, the explosion of joy as you watch the sea part!

So it was for the People of God, and so it is for us.

There is always the fearful wait, then a sudden light.

The wait is yours, the light is God's.

And it is free.

You can never claim you have deserved it.

On the contrary!

No merit has the power to open the door.

Only God's love freely given can manage this impassable lock.

'When he closes, nobody can open' (Revelation 3.7).

But his will is always prompt to open for 'This is why I came into the world, so that they can have life and have it to the full' (John 10.10).

How often have you asked, 'Why am I still here?'

And the reply is always the same.

You must learn to love. For beyond the door there is nothing – except love.

I personally like to think of a city, a feast, a choir singing great sacred music. It matters that you're there and yet it doesn't matter that you're there. That is for me a particularly good picture of heaven. And I have to put beside that the bit in Revelation about God giving us the white stone which just has the name on it, which nobody else knows except you and God (Revelation 2.17). The other thing I think is that the gates of the city are on all four sides, so that wherever you start from, there is an open gateway waiting for you. Never forgetting that however joyous the end, dying itself is hard work.

In terms of the practical side of my work, I'm always learning. We're always learning. I try to keep up to date on the clinical side; I don't see patients any more unless they ask for me, but I'm learning to appreciate their creativity and all that goes on in our day centre. At the end of the day, we're committed to giving the best possible care to the terminally ill. Although St Christopher's is a Christian foundation, we welcome people of any, or of no, faith. For me, however, I believe that God revealed in Christ shared and shares the darkness of suffering and dying, and it is this belief that is behind my work to transform the reality of death.

5

The West Family

In August 1993, the Wests lost their son, David. He was twenty-eight years old when he died from leukemia.

Ken West is a service engineer and his wife, Cathy, works part time in the local bakery. The family has lived in Oxfordshire for thirty-five years; their three children were born between 1962 and 1971. The eldest, Debbie, is married with two children. The youngest, Christopher, lives at home and works in the gardens of an Oxford college.

David worked for the BBC. After studying the technical aspects of broadcasting, he went on to pursue a career in local radio. In 1992, he achieved his ambition of becoming a radio presenter, hosting a daily afternoon programme.

KEN:

It was in May 1992 that we first knew David was ill. He began to be very tired.

CATHY:

In the mornings, he would wake up feeling sick. He'd come into the sitting-room for about half an hour, and after a cup of tea he was all right. To begin with I thought it was a virus; but he had one terrible weekend.

KEN:

It was a fine weekend and we were in the garden. I remember I came in here and he was just lying on the settee. The colour of his face was terrible – almost yellow. We just had no idea.

CATHY:

And he wouldn't go to the doctor, until one night when he had a very bad throat. The doctor took one look at him, did a blood test, and then gave him a letter to the hospital. He went the next day and had a blood transfusion; the tests had shown that he had leukemia.

KEN:

But it didn't sink in. We didn't know anything about leukemia; we knew that it was an illness that children had, but that was all really. We didn't know what it was going to mean.

CHRISTOPHER:

I couldn't believe it. It was the word – leukemia. He knew before we did and when he told Mum and Dad, he said 'Sit down. I've got something to tell you.' He broke the news like that.

KEN:

I can remember the feeling … I think it was the next morning, when I got up and had a wash and a shave. I just broke down. The sudden realization that he was seriously ill. But it seemed better for a while after that, because David kept on working. He kept everything inside; he didn't say a lot. He knew it was serious, but he never liked to upset us, and so nothing much was talked about and certainly in the early stages he didn't want us to tell anybody.

For the first few months, it was simply a question of blood transfusions, and he used to go on a Sunday whenever he could. Nobody knew at work, so he tried to fit it in outside his hours.

CATHY:

He would come home after work and he'd just pop his head round to say hello before going straight upstairs to his room. He'd close the bedroom door and we'd think perhaps he'd had a bad day at work. He didn't say anything to us, but when we look back now, we think he was probably exhausted.

KEN:

The blood transfusions were about every six weeks, and towards the end of each period, he'd be so tired and would go this sort of yellow colour. Then he'd ring up the hospital and go in.

CHRISTOPHER:

Whenever he had a transfusion, he came home a completely different person.

KEN:

Yes! Just like recharging batteries – he was alive again, and it was almost an immediate effect.

But then, of course, the subject of the bone-marrow transplant came up. We thought the ideal donor would be either Christopher or Debbie, but neither of them were really suitable. So we had to put our names on a list and wait for the right match. The matching service is amazing; nowadays a donor might come from the other side of the world, whereas at one time it was just this country. In the meantime, we just went from transfusion to transfusion.

Then we were told they'd found a donor, which was marvellous. We didn't know how it was done – I always imagined a bone-marrow transplant having something to do with the bone itself. But it's a reddish colour, not unlike blood.

CATHY:

It's not an operation as such; it's more like a transfusion. I think it's worse for the donor because the bone marrow is taken from the spine and they get rather bruised.

KEN:

Then David said to Cathy that he wasn't going to go through with it and that was a bit distressing – for you, Cathy. You didn't tell me until the following day.

CATHY:

I was hoping he'd change his mind, you see.

KEN:

And I was thinking: 'Well, he's got this chance; he can't let this chance go.' And David's attitude was 'It's my life. I can do what I like.'

CATHY:

Well, what if things went wrong? That was what was in his mind. If he'd been sure everything was going to go well, there'd have been no problem. But there can never be any guarantee. He was frightened.

KEN:

Yes … but we did have this little bit of an upset. We didn't come to any agreement that night, but then he said the next day that he would go through with it. It turned out that he had to go to the Royal Marsden Hospital in Surrey, because the donor was a student with only one week after her exams before she left the country.

He told a couple of people at work and went into hospital in July 1993. And there's one day – that terrible day – I'll never forget. I just go back to July 10th every year. It was when he last walked out of this house. You know, you still think of things like that. Last year, when I was upstairs decorating, I was working in his bedroom: all the children used to write things on the wall in pencil and so when I took the paper off – it was there. David's writing.

CATHY:

And I remember him saying as he left, 'You'll keep my room, won't you?'

KEN:

He wasn't actually admitted to the hospital until five o'clock in the evening and so we went to get a pizza, I remember. David said then, 'I wonder if there's a park we could walk in.' I had a sense that he didn't really want to go to the hospital.

CHRISTOPHER:

I wanted to go in with him, but he didn't want me to. He was like that. But he didn't even say he'd see me another day.

CATHY:

He had all his emotions inside; he didn't want to show it.

We used to visit at the weekend and once during the week. Down the M25 – I can't hear that word now without being reminded of those awful trips. I hate that road. Our son-in-law used to take us in the week and he really was so good. He's been just like a son to us.

KEN:

Everything appeared to have gone well with the transplant, except that he got an infection. He developed big cysts under his arm, but we never found out why that happened. We've had regrets that we never asked and we were never told.

CATHY:

We just trusted the doctors and thought everything would be fine.

KEN:

Once he'd had the chemotherapy, we had to stay outside the room.

Everything we took in had to be sterilized and then when we could go in, we had to have sterile clothing from head to toe. But we didn't have any masks and we couldn't understand that. He must have been open to infection like that. It was terrible really – I sensed how he was feeling; I remember he looked at me through the window with such a look on his face – 'Take me out of here,' he seemed to be saying.

This went on for a few weeks and then, at the beginning of August, he rang us on a Wednesday evening and said 'I don't think I'm going to make it, Dad.' And I was a little bit like I am – you know, 'Of course you are, David. You'll fight this, you know you will.' I'd always admired him in his fight to get the work he wanted, because lots of things were against him. But when I rang the nurse to find out, she said she wasn't worried. And then she told David we'd rung and he rang back, a little bit annoyed, and asked what all the fuss was about.

CATHY:

I could understand, because it must have made him think he was worse than perhaps he hoped. And we didn't ever want to worry him.

KEN:

And then he rang back again to say sorry. Even though he was that ill, he rang to say he was sorry for upsetting us.

CATHY:

He never liked to upset anybody. If he ever thought he'd upset you, he'd come in every now and then and say 'Are you all right?'

KEN:

Then on the Thursday the hospital rang and asked if we could come in that day. I came home from work and Jo, our son-in-law, borrowed his boss's car and took us up there. At first we thought it was going to be all right, because the doctor told us that he was out of the critical state and that his blood count had gone up.

CATHY:
And we could go in! Without getting dressed up.

KEN:
So we went in, but poor old David was struggling then on the oxygen. He was on pure oxygen, which was a bit strange we thought. His chest was going up and down, he was hot, he couldn't hold a conversation.

CATHY:
He couldn't eat or drink and the doctor had to put some moisturizer on his lips because they were so dry. That part of it stays in our mind and it was awful. Then in the afternoon, David's blood count went down again and we were called into the doctor's office. He told us then they were pessimistic.

We sat there all evening. Christopher and Debbie came up. The nurse told us to get some sleep, but we couldn't sleep and really we wished we had stayed.

KEN:
Then the next thing was early morning and we heard footsteps coming up the corridor. This may sound strange, but it was almost as if they were coming for me. There was a tap on the door and as I opened it, two nurses came in. They said 'We've got some bad news: David stopped breathing about half an hour ago.'

Your world sort of falls apart. You just don't know where you are. It's so devastating. And you think all sorts of things – like we weren't there with him. That's the big regret.

We asked for the chaplain and he walked us down to the

hospital chapel – and there again, this terrible feeling. And we sat in the chapel on our own for a while.

CATHY:

I think the worst walk though was from the chapel to the ward, where David still was. That was awful.

KEN:

The awful thing was that David was never baptized. That was partly my fault. I feel very guilty about this. We had Debbie baptized, but David and Christopher weren't. I should have pushed it and I'll carry that guilt all the way. You see, I was brought up in the Catholic faith and if you weren't baptized, you never went to heaven. You went into limbo.

But we were stuck. We couldn't ask the chaplain to baptize David the day before, because David was so alert in his mind and we couldn't do that to him. We couldn't frighten David. But the chaplain told me that his church – the Anglican church – doesn't believe that. He couldn't actually baptize him, but after he died, he did bless him and put a cross on his forehead.

When we went to see him, all the hospital paraphernalia had been taken away and he was just lying there. I've never said this to anybody, but to see one's own child – son – lying there having just died ... well, I don't think there's anything quite like it. Anything quite as devastating.

CHRISTOPHER:
He looked so exhausted, so worn out.

CATHY:

We were in such a state of shock. We just sat in the room. They did ask us if they could do a post-mortem, to see what effect the drugs had had. We said yes, because we thought if we could help someone else, that would be good. But even then, we didn't sort David's things out properly. They just brought two bags in.

We really didn't know what we were doing. Debbie and Jo went to register his death, while we sat in the car.

KEN:

You're sort of numb, but in a strange way I wanted to be doing things. We had to arrange the funeral straightaway – that same afternoon. You have to tell them all the details, even down to choosing the coffin. You look at a catalogue of coffins – I know you've got to do it, but it's the same day!

Then there was a mix-up with the funeral dates. They didn't do the post-mortem when they said they were going to and we had to change the day at the last minute. So he was buried on Friday August 13th, 1993. But the family and all his friends were there. It meant so much to us to have all of his friends there – many of whom we'd never met before and some of whom we've kept in touch with. One of David's friends, Chris Phillips, spoke at the funeral and we played David's favourite song.

CATHY:

The song we played, 'Meet on the Ledge' by Fairport Convention, was the last song he played on the radio before he went into hospital. We didn't know that.

CHRISTOPHER:

Before he went into hospital, he said half-jokingly to me, 'If ever I go or anything, I'd like this song to be played at my funeral.' We used to listen to it together.

KEN:

We sat together one afternoon and played the tape and the tears were streaming down our faces. It was the words: he was on his way up, the air was thin, he would meet all his friends. And we put a copy of that tape in with him in the coffin. Another piece he liked was 'From a Distance', which Fairport Convention also did.

We had a lot of support from people around that time and I was quite overwhelmed really. We didn't really know David's friends and in a way we were learning a lot more about him.

Then I suppose the realization gradually dawned on us. I used to wake up in the morning and for a split second would be fine, and then the memory would come flooding back. We used to talk so much – for weeks and weeks.

CATHY:

We were very lucky really. I think something like this can split families up.

KEN:

Possibly because they don't talk. But we still refer to David as though he's around. He is part of the family. We had three children, not two. We still think of three.

We never had any offers of counselling. I suppose we could have gone out and found it, but, to be honest, I didn't want it.

CATHY:

I would have liked it, but not in a group. Only one-to-one. We did have one friend, though, who helped us a lot.

KEN:

Not many people want to listen. They want to go on about themselves. I think that's one thing something like this teaches you. It does teach you to listen.

If anything could turn people away from their faith, from God, it would be something like losing your child. But it did the opposite for us. I had to go on thinking and believing that David was out there, and I want him to be happy and at peace. And we do feel that.

CATHY:

I think we all feel that. And I'm not embarrassed about talking about my faith now. I think a lot of people do feel embarrassed about talking about religion or their faith. I can talk to other people who might be going through something similar and talk about the things that have helped me.

KEN:

I was talking to someone the other day about families and children. He told me that his parents never gave him a cuddle or whatever and I said how strange that was, because mine never did either. And it's so important. He said his Dad has never turned round to him and said he loves him. I think we were brought up like that. I think the last time I gave Debbie a hug was when we found out she was expecting Laura – I think she was a bit embarrassed, but I was so pleased for her and I wanted to!

CATHY:

I think we are a much closer family now. We do this sort of thing more now. It changes your outlook on life.

KEN:

People do ask if we'll ever get over it. It's difficult to say. It's not such a big hurt, but it's always there. Everybody gets highs and lows in life; some go deeper and higher than others, but when we're down, the whole business goes through our minds and we pick out bits. And that hurt and sadness will never go. It doesn't really get better.

CATHY:

It helps to know that we're going to see him again. We all die. We tend to forget that. But even though he's not here in his body, the fact he's dead doesn't seem real. I sometimes feel as if he's really there. I suppose we are lucky because we have some of the tapes of his programmes, so we can hear his voice and it's just as it used to be, when we would hear him over the radio.

KEN:

I don't think the hurt will ever go away. Every so often, just for a few seconds, you get all these emotions – disbelief, anger. I don't know whether that will ever go away.

CHRISTOPHER:

I think it is worse for you because you're his parents. I do miss him, but I don't feel angry or ask 'Why did it happen to us?' Why anyone? It sometimes hits me, but mostly I have happy thoughts and memories of David and feel he's around now, listening to our thoughts.

You have to take a giant step back from the perspective of life and look on a profound level. It's an experience. I often feel I don't fit in with life, but David's departure has broadened my views. I think there is a reason for who I am. Although it is a great loss, maybe it has helped me feel proud to be an individual. Some good can come out of things like this.

CATHY:

I think it's faith that keeps you going. I mean, Mary lost Jesus, didn't she? She lost her son and he suffered, didn't he? She must have had the same feelings and I often think of her.

KEN:

We know he can't come back, but what we want is the knowledge that he's happy and at peace. And if he gets that from being with God, then I think that is part of the joy.

I always thought that hell wasn't fire and damnation as such. It's that when you die, you see almighty God and then you're sent away. That is the tortuous part. Then you have to work your way back to him.

CATHY:

And the more sins you've got, the further down the pit you go and the longer it takes to climb up again. But you can climb.

In fact, I felt I was in a pit when I lost David. And I've had to climb. It's not really a question of time – people say one year, two years. No. It's something else. It's learning to cope. You go down so far, and on the way back up, you slip back several times; you slip back into utter despair. But each time you climb again, you climb a bit higher. And the more times you climb the same bit, the easier that bit becomes. Slowly, you get used to it.

6

Ngakpa Chögyam Rinpoche and Khandro Déchen

Ngakpa Chögyam Rinpoche and his wife, Khandro Déchen, are Spiritual Directors of Sang-ngak-cho-dzong, a Buddhist charity based in South Wales. They are Buddhist Lamas whose teaching work focuses on birth, death and relationship. From the Buddhist perspective, it is not possible to speak of death without speaking of birth. The one falls into the other, as naturally as the cycle of breathing. The many opportunities in life, therefore, to understand the nature of death are seen as preparation material for the final outbreath of this existence, the birth into the Unknown.

Ngakpa Rinpoche is the incarnation of Aro Yeshe, a Tibetan yogi and son of the female visionary genius, Khyungchen Aro Lingma. He trained in India, following Tibetan Buddhist Lineages on the teachings of Nyingma Inner Tantra. He returned to the West in 1982 and now lives in South Wales. Khandro Déchen is a former Macmillan nurse, specializing in advising and counselling the terminally ill in their homes.

NGAKPA RINPOCHE:

The first thing to say is that the association of life and death as polarities is not a Buddhist concept. The pairing we prefer is birth and death. Birth and death happen continually; they are processes within life.

Our approach to working with people is to introduce them to the births and deaths within their lives, rather than looking at death as something which is going to happen at some point in the future. From our perspective, you can't really relate with death as a physical event unless you can relate with the death that happens in every moment. We tend to look at death as the end of a particular period; we talk about the word 'bardo'. Bardo is usually a word that is used in connection with the space between one rebirth and another rebirth – the period in which visions occur. But there are many other ways of using this word. Bardo actually means gap, space, or transition. It is easier to relate with the larger bardos of life – for example: the bardo of infancy; the bardo of childhood; and the bardo of adolescence. These periods have flavours, and we have a sense that they begin and end. Photographs are very interesting; I find that I can look at photographs of when I was a child but I can't remember who I was. I can remember the thoughts and ideas, but the emotional texture of that time is gone.

I think my most intense experience of death was being in solitary retreat. My first solitary retreat was three months in a hut up in the Himalayan mountains of northern India. It was very traumatic at first. I had been instructed to go into this retreat by my teacher, who was rather like 'the good father' to me, and we had had a very happy relationship. When I went into retreat, it just seemed like the next thing to do, but then the horror of being on my own in a hut up in the mountains; and of having nothing with which I could relate. I started thinking about the past and projecting into the future, which worked for a while by occupying me during the times when I wasn't engaged in formal practice. But the longer I was in retreat, the more unreal the past became and the more unreal the future became: there's something about making plans that involves some physical contact with the beginning of a process. Take a simple example: I'm going to put up a shelf. I can see the wall and see where on the wall I will put the shelf. I may not put up the shelf until next week, but I can plan the stages required. But when there is no physical contact, you can't invest a lot in it because it's too far in the future.

So, in the end, you have to give up thinking about the future and the past, because instead of becoming more and more rich, they become more and more dead. All you've got is the present moment, and if you particularly don't like the present moment, then that's not fun at all; in fact it can be quite horrific. What happened to me, after a great deal of tears and complicated plans of how I could leave or pretend to be ill – an incredible welter of neuroses and paranoia – I finally thought, 'Well, if I'm not going to stay here, this is something that is going to colour the rest of my life. I'm going to be a person who backs out of things. I don't really want to set up that pattern for myself, so I've got to stay here.' The only way I could endure staying there was to think 'That's it. I'm in here for ever.' As soon as I made that decision, it was fine. Suddenly it was all right to be there.

The impact of that experience has remained with me ever since. It remained with me throughtout the three years of retreat I subsequently completed. I don't need company any more. If I have it, it's very nice and I enjoy it, but I no longer need it.

This has interesting implications when we think about the nature of memory. If someone has amnesia, or senile dementia, are they still alive or have they died? In a Buddhist constuct, you die and are reborn into a new body, and in the new body you have forgotten all previous lives. Without memory, the world as we know it becomes an unreliable place. There are no recognizable reference points.

There is one Lama in India in fact who is to all intents and purposes senile, but it has no effect on him really. He can't remember the names of the monks who serve him, but he still teaches. He doesn't rely on memory for the teaching; teaching is the moment-to-moment reality he talks about and so there is no problem. Being trapped in that moment of not knowing, of not having any memory, is either delightful or terrible.

KHANDRO DÉCHEN

Buddhism is a very different philosophy from the one we practise in the West. I worked in acute cancer care, where the emphasis was very much on getting the person better, curing them. I really didn't feel completely at home with that because I thought that the inevitability of death for patients – whether it was a year, two years, ten years – was neglected in favour of the rushing around trying to get them their treatment on time, to give them the right drugs at the right time. Acute oncology care is very demanding, for both staff and patients. So I ended up working in hospice care and came here to Penarth, where I spent a very intensive six months working with a Consultant. She was a very powerful personality and I watched her a lot whenever she was talking to people.

The strange thing was that death was hardly ever talked about. I found that throughout my year in dealing with people who were dying, there were very few people who could even let that awareness in. They were more concerned with evading the issue, and showed real avoidance behaviour. For example, I would sometimes be with a doctor, telling a person what was wrong with them, what the consequences of that were and what the likely outcome was going to be. Then when we left the room, we would hear the person telling somebody else a completely different version of what we had been talking about. I've learnt a lot from that and it's fascinated me how we all have our own, often very different, versions of reality. Very few people wanted to talk about death, even though we were available if they wanted to talk about it. That really surprised me.

I also worked as a community Macmillan nurse in the South

Wales valley, and in those sorts of communities, death has always been a bigger part of life. People there have had less opportunity really to escape it with the coal-mining disasters, the poverty, the low standard of child health. Yet, even there, there was still a lot of avoidance in the time leading up to death. There was a greater acceptance of the actual death, because the person would often die at home and be laid out in an open coffin in the parlour. You probably don't see that anywhere else now except in such rural communities. But still, there was avoidance.

To be honest, I'm not sure what influence the hospice movement really has had on this aspect of death. The people who could deal with death were those who had a spiritual belief system: one that was very strong, and which they'd had most of their life. You can't suddenly give someone that. You do hear of the odd person who has a spiritual experience in the last stages of their life, but I found those people very rarely. Certainly the physical care, the time and the opportunity to try out other things, like acupuncture or massage, makes a difference, but as far as the openness goes when it comes to talking about death, about what it's going to feel like, what is going to happen after death – that was virtually non-existent.

And it's not something I would ever push on someone. My own belief is that you go as far as people want to go. You don't project them out of denial because denial might be healthy for them if they haven't got any other support system within themselves.

This level of denial tends to run throughout our lives. We don't deal with disjuncture or crisis, the deaths that we have all the way through our lives. Divorce, for instance. The end of a relationship. Those sorts of disjunctures in our lives disturb us greatly. Unless you actually look for, welcome and embrace those disjunctures in your life, you can never learn to accept them. I don't mean you have to accept them calmly – you can live them and scream them. There's a lot of talk about 'relaxing into death', which I find nauseating. Great if you can, but it is far better to be yourself.

NGAKPA RINPOCHE:

Khandro Déchen and I have been teaching together now for about two years. I have been formally teaching for twelve years, and informally for nineteen years. I was asked to come back to the West by my teachers in India and I started by teaching at the local Buddhist centre in Cardiff.

I had no clear idea at that stage how my life as a teacher was going to evolve, but it is mainly the theme of integration that I have evolved. Many people have a very romantic idea of the Eastern traditions. So our concern is to integrate these particular teachings into the ordinary daily lives of Western people. Ours is not a celibate or monastic tradition. So we have students who are married, and who also have families. Birth and death are part of every aspect of teaching: they're part of meditation, they're part of communication and relationship.

I remember one talk in particular that I was invited to give. There were a lot of questions about how to be with dying people. I asked 'Who are these dying people? Are you saying that we are not dying people? Say I go to visit my "dying" friend in hospital who is dying, and I walk out of the hospital and am killed by a car as I cross the road. Who was the dying person?' We're all dying people and we're all heading in that direction. It's purely a matter of time, so where do you place that point? The final diagnosis? The moment the pain starts? It's completely arbitrary and therefore you can't talk to a person who is not dying, because we're all dying. What you're really saying is that you can't talk to people. The difficulty you experience in talking to an obviously dying person comes from a tendency to talk only about 'doing' things, especially things that refer to the future. If you're the sort of person who can only talk in that way, of course you become very embarrassed and feel stuck about what to talk about.

I remember being in a hospice room with someone who had perhaps only a week left. I took an object out of my bag and started to talk about it with her; we then talked about the colour shadows on the wall made by the cheeseplant. I said that people rarely look at things like that. I said that most people don't see how *green* a shadow can be. There was a general feeling of irritation in the room. When I made these comments I got the sense that people thought I was talking about trivia. But if you think about it, if you're dying, all you've got is what is in the room, and if *that* is trivial, then your last moment of life will be trivial.

This example brings us to the Buddhist understanding of the five elements and the sensing fields. If your sense fields are open and alive, you can enjoy them up to the moment they dissolve. You can enjoy the fact that the blind is green, simply because it is green. And if it's not enjoyable now, when you die, you know you're going to get nothing from that blind, nothing from the ceiling, nothing from the carpet. They're not going to feed you in any way. That is terrible!

What happens to you when you die depends on the practice you've done in your life and here we could talk about Dream Yoga. Dying is more or less the same as going to sleep. There is a process of dissolution of the elements. The first dissolution is a level of experience to which most people can relate: it is when the earth element dissolves into the water element. These words 'earth' and 'water' refer to the physical states as well as to the psychological, esoteric states. What actually happens, in terms of experience, can be likened to the experience of falling asleep. Imagine it takes five or so minutes to fall asleep. In that interim period between lying down and being asleep, my body will become vague. I appear to drift in and out of consciousness. That's the earth element dissolving into the water element. The water element then dissolves into the fire element, into the air element, into the space element. The space element then dissolves into itself and there is the realization of the clear light. That is the empty nature of being, which you may or may not recognize, depending on your awareness. If you reject it, then you go into the visions, which are rather like the dreams you have when you are asleep.

The Bardo Thödröl Chenmo, known as 'The Tibetan Book of the Dead', is only called that because there is an 'Egyptian Book of the Dead' that was known about before. 'Thödröl' means liberation through hearing, through perceiving.

The visions that are described in the book are not there for everybody. They are only there for the people who have practised those visualizations. Everyone has visions, but those visions are karmic visions and depend on our lives. They also depend on our spiritual tradition. Not everyone is going to see Buddha figures, because that practice is one of relating to one's own energy in symbolic form and one has to have done that within one's life. If you're very familiar with those vibrations, it transposes everything that arises into a 'deiform' context. But most people experience themselves rather like they experience themselves in their dreams. They go straight into the pattern of their consciousness, and that can be radically affected by what happens in the moment of death or just before. Which is why it's not a good idea to feel anger just before you die. The state of mind in which you enter the death process carries through. I feel this is why confession is stressed within the Christian tradition. That's really important, because with forgiveness and absolution, you enter a more peaceful state.

But this is also true within our lives. Whatever circumstances you experience, your frame of mind will colour it. If you go to a party in a bad mood, that colours your whole experience. It's important to realize that death is no different from life. Death *is* life. It's another phase of life, and what you experience in death is not so different from what you experienced in life.

The time it takes before you enter another body is described in the texts as forty-nine days, but days don't mean much when you don't have a physical body. When you leave the physical earth, there is no such thing as time any more. It's better to describe it as forty-nine phases, and to go through those may take someone hours, weeks, years, decades …

You have choice, and yet no choice, when it comes to where you go – rather like life. I see an olive and I can eat it or not eat it; but in fact I have no choice because I don't like olives. That's both choice and no-choice at the same time. The practice of Buddhism is a practice of expanding your capacity for choice in the direction of compassion.

Buddhism doesn't talk about aiming to avoid rebirth. That idea comes more from some Hindu systems. It is referred to in Buddhism, but what is actually meant is that *compulsory* rebirth is transcended. Let me go back to the example I gave of being in solitary retreat. Before that experience, I had a compulsive need for company. It isn't so much that I have transcended the enjoyment of company, that I can now live in a cave and never see anyone. I still enjoy people, I enjoy them very much. But if they're not there, I don't *suffer*.

In terms of Buddhism, there are different vehicles for transcendence. They are Sutra, Tantra and Dzogchen. Sutra is largely the monastic approach and is a path of renunciation; Tantra is an approach that utilizes energy and is a path of transformation. Dzogchen is a path of self-liberation; which is not 'liberation for myself', but 'of itself it liberates itself'. The image that's given is of a snake uncoiling its own knot. What is the knot? What is the snake? Where has the knot gone when it is unknotted? Are the knot and the snake different?

From the perspective of both Tantra and Dzogchen, having a body is not a problem. Living in the world is not a problem. That is why it's not a celibate order. Enlightenment isn't seen as an escape from the earth, as if the earth was a problem. From that perspective, 'samsara' – suffering – is simply duality; it's not the world. It is a question of *how* you live and how you perceive life. From this perspective, there is emptiness. From emptiness, energy arises and from energy, form arises. Form then dissolves back into energy, which dissolves back into emptiness. That is continually happening, and has no end.

From the point of view of Sutra, which defines the basic human problem as attachment to form, it emphasizes emptiness. Within that system of teaching, one can get the idea that the world and the body are a burden.

The idea with enlightenment is not that you don't take rebirth again, but that neurotic compulsion to be incarnated doesn't impel you to grasp it regardless of the outcome. You're not striving for it, because you have to have it in order to feel real: you're equally as real in any condition.

One could make an analogy here with what Khandro Déchen was saying earlier about divorce. One can be real in the marriage, real in the process of divorce and real afterwards when one has established another relationship. Most people tend not to feel real during the divorce process, when one thing is dissolving out of being and nothing yet has arisen. A lot of people will want another relationship very quickly in order to feel real again. Obviously, if you're more free than that, you can feel real without entering quickly into another relationship and you are better able to make a choice based on attraction rather than a choice based on compulsion.

Attraction can be something spontaneous or it can be complicated. It can be 'you're near enough; I could alter you, change this, take that away …'. That's not really attraction at all; that's neediness.

We give teaching on relationship as well as on birth and death, because the sphere of Tantric Buddhism is completely interpenetrating; interengulfing. Relationship is crucial at every level;

male–female relationship, relationship with friends, relationship of yourself to your life, your surroundings, your ideas, your wants, your anxieties, your dreams. Relationship is very important in Tantra and the analogy of relationship applies to everything. Tantra is a vehicle of Buddhism that is not spoken of as much as Sutra.

KHANDRO DÉCHEN:

One of the ideas of Tantra is that of experiencing the empty or death quality within relationship. Accepting that it could end at any moment, and so living it fully while it is there. That isn't to say you can't have commitment, but commitment doesn't mean making something concrete out of it. When you make something concrete out of your relationship, you start to walk all over it, stop respecting it, take it for granted. That's always something people have to watch.

Tantra talks about how to keep the initial attraction alive, the romance. It sees romance as a spiritual experience. It is possible to stay in love for ever if you encourage the spiritual side of a relationship. The kindness and the openness that you have at the beginning of a relationship, when you're not sure if this person is going to stay, so you really have to do everything possible to make them stay – and you make yourself a very nice person – *that* is a phase that is enormously spiritually potent.

NGAKPA RINPOCHE:

There is a lot of very unromantic advice about relationships around at the moment. We saw one book recently that said 'Falling in love is a relatively harmless pathology, after which the real work of a relationship begins.'

I found it depressing that this is the latest knowledge that people have about relationship. I can understand it completely, but it's very depressing. Having a wonderful relationship should be something people can have relatively simply. Not easily, but simply.

The mechanics of it are very easy to explain. The method of remaining in a wonderful relationship is very simple. Somehow falling in love and romance project you into an experience with enormous spiritual potential, and to stay there you have to allow openness and kindness, wisdom and compassion, to keep manifesting. (Openness refers to an openness *to*, rather than an openness about.) Remember how willing you were at the beginning of a relationship to go to Scotland for the weekend – tired? Well, never mind. Keep *that* alive.

Tantra espouses the idea of relationship in everything we do. Having a good relationship involves the same level of appreciation as enjoying a good meal, enjoying the emptying of your bowels, enjoying a good death. Whatever you do is interesting, pleasurable or at least open-ended in some way. You know, you cut your finger and it hurts, but is pain all there is? Is there perhaps something else as well?

Neither Khandro Déchen nor I like the somewhat prissy idea of 'If you're dying and you know it, clap your hands'. There is a lot of sadness in death. But that sadness doesn't have to be negative in terms of loss. It certainly is sad when you lose contact with somebody, when you know that you're not going to be able to relate in this way again. But the kind of death that occurs in a happy relationship, where many different phases are acknowledged, feels different. People grow in different directions and in order to follow someone, you have to die. You have to die in order to stay with them. You lose something, but you don't mind because the relationship is worthwhile. People often feel that if something is not going to be there for ever – guaranteed – they can't enjoy it. We feel that really affects the period leading up to death, the idea that 'because I'm going to die, I can't enjoy anything now'.

This leads me to the the idea of possession. Sometimes we behave in relationships as if we possess the other person. But, in fact, when can you even own an object? Really it is only while you are enjoying it. When it is out of the room, do you still own it? It's not only when it's stolen that you no longer own it, but when you no longer care for it. If you have some object that you no longer care for, do you still own it? If someone else legally owns it, can you say you don't own it? If you're looking at it and enjoying it, you own it more than someone who legally owns it. It seems enjoyment is more a qualifying factor of ownership than legal ownership. That applies to relationship as well. It applies to dying. It applies to being born. It applies to life.

By enjoyment we mean appreciation, which means contact and communication, which means compassion. Compassion is communication; it's not having a barrier between two things. In Tantric language, enjoyment, appreciation, communication, compassion are all the same energy. So, having an appreciative death has the same meaning as compassion: you're not cut off. You have compassion for yourself, for others; you have connection with everything.

7

The Reverend James Woodward

James Woodward is a hospital chaplain at the Queen Elizabeth Hospital in Birmingham. He is also author of two books in the area of death and dying: *Embracing the Chaos: Theological Reflections on AIDS* (1990); and *Encountering Illness: Voices in Pastoral and Theological Perspective* (1995).

After an undergraduate degree in theology, James Woodward spent some time working at St Christopher's Hospice in Sydenham. He then trained for ministry at Westcott House, Cambridge, and was ordained in the Anglican Church, serving his title at Consett Parish Church. His own upbringing in a mining community in north-east England had shown him a naturalness about death. During his past ten years of ministry he has been involved in the activity of pastoral care in a variety of settings. In his writing he has attempted to confront prejudice and ignorance through a creative dialogue between theology and experience.

A very formative experience which has shaped part of my attitude around working with the dying goes back to my childhood. I was born and brought up in a small mining village in County Durham. It was a working-class community, which demonstrated healthy attitudes in dealing with death and dying. One of my earliest memories is of my great-grandmother dying; I remember being very much part of the process by which the family said goodbye to her and grieved. I remember my grandmother going to get the sheets that the village used to lay out people, and I remember people coming to lay her out and talking about it as they were doing it – I cannot have been much older than six or seven – the undertakers bringing the coffin to the house, and my great-grandmother's body standing under the living-room window. I remember the family gathering around, talking about Gran, and a relative lifting me up to see her so I could touch her face and say goodbye.

There was no fear. There was grief, sadness and that strange dislocated feeling that comes with endings and beginnings, but I understand now that there was a kind of facing of the reality of what was going on. I don't know what effect that had on me in my spiritual journey but it is a very important guiding picture as I think about death and dying.

In 1979, I went on to read theology at London University. This was part of finding myself drawn into the Church and faith as an activity where things were explained; life was understood, and human experience was interpreted. In those teenage years, there was a very powerful sense of the Church and its worship being the bridge holding and connecting aspects of life; a place that showed me that there was a deep sense of meaning and purpose in life.

I was an explorer, asking questions and searching for answers, and very much wanted to make sense of what was going on inside me as well as around me. Quite by chance, over lunch after a Sunday service during the run-up to my finals, I met someone who worked at St Christopher's Hospice and he asked me what I was thinking of doing. I had by this time decided to proceed with exploring my vocation and he told me of the system whereby ordinands can be employed as nursing auxilliaries for a year or so at St Christopher's. I don't know whether that childhood experience had any effect, but the nursing felt attractive and I felt that I'd really like to do this.

So, between 1982 and 1983 I spent a year at St Christopher's, with a whole number of ordinands and people in ministry. The most amazing thing about St Christopher's is the huge number of people that the institution and its philosophy has touched. And so I arrived, a rather young undergraduate, but I suppose fairly thoughtful and reflective for my age. Really it was there that many things began to happen for me, which laid the groundwork for everything I've done in my ministry since.

Above all, I was forced to face my own vulnerability, humanity, mortality, weakness and fear, and to accept these as part of what it means to be a human being. There is still a huge part of me that is fairly fearful about dying. I don't think that my experience at the hospice or since has taken away the fundamental sense that at a basic level I'd rather like to live for ever. I don't find it easy to embrace the ambiguities and uncertainties of life, but the hospice taught me that the key to living was to do that – to face one's dying, to face the mystery at the heart of an authentic and integrated human life story. The people who taught me that were in fact mostly the people whom I nursed.

I think the uniqueness of the hospice situation, which I've never experienced since, was the authenticity of the encounter. It was also about my receptivity as a human being. It was simply one human being encountering another human being. One of the dangers of modern culture is that it builds and organizes things around professional boundaries, rather than authentic human encounters. There is something about the professionalism of the doctor, the nurse, the chaplain, the priest that actually imposes a self-protecting distance. There was an honesty with the people I nursed. I'm sure I said lots of things to them I should never have said, but also I think it can be genuinely helpful if you can simply say as naturally as possible what's going on in that space between you, if you can articulate what's going on in your head and heart.

On reflection perhaps it gave an authenticity and humanity to the encounter that I think I've lost in the process of becoming a pastoral professional. One learns to become more detached, to control one's tears, one's fears, and it can be very difficult with a dog collar to say to people 'I don't know' when they demand an answer from you. And there are times when all of us have to say 'I don't know', 'I haven't got the answer.'

It's important as well not to be too serious about it. A lot of the encounters were not about dying, but about living as fully as possible in the present. There was a lot of gossip, a lot of reflection, sharing about family relationships, interests, just chatting about whatever the day had brought. It was a very wonderful mixture that shaped my theology and spirituality.

Over the past six years I've worked as a hospital chaplain in Birmingham: I can honestly say that I don't know what it is that makes some encounters work and others not work. It's nothing to do with time. You can spend ten minutes with someone and it can be transforming, or you can spend hours with another person and nothing appears to happen. I'm not sure what conditions one needs to create around which authenticity, connectedness, meaning and depth can become part of the space between you and the other person. It may be to do with one's own receptivity and sensitivity.

Another thing I can share with you which comes out of my experience of HIV/AIDS and hospital chaplaincy is that life is rather messy. Life is complicated, problematic, difficult, uncontrollable, fragile and unpredictable. So I don't believe there can ever really be a pattern to the process of dying, a recognizable series of stages to dying. I take on board all the psychological writings around the stages of dying – denial, anger, grief, acceptance – but I've never seen anyone adhere to the pattern and work through them all. All of us bring to our living and dying such a rich and complex mixture of things. I think we need to resist the desire for a pattern or be careful about the process of interpretation, because it can be a way of exercising control over something that is ultimately uncontrollable.

I feel rather that it's about people being themselves in the situation; being present, open and honest. We talk a lot about a death-denying society, but actually most people just get on and do it. It's visiting time in the hospital now, for instance, and I'm sure there are lots of people attending to each other in different ways. There will be, perhaps, a partner sitting by the bed, reading the newspaper, and there is an authenticity, a faithfulness and honesty about that encounter, which there may not be from a nurse who wants to counsel the patient into a psychological acceptance of their condition. That's a bit of a generalization, but it makes a point.

I preached on Advent Sunday this year back in my first parish in the North-East. Traditionally, the Church thinks about the four last things during Advent, one of which is death. I was preaching about death and I wanted the sermon to be very practical. I told the congregation that I felt it was very important that that week they had a conversation about dying with one of their neighbours, because they needed to be honest and open about what their fears were around dying. Another thing I asked them to do, which I feel passionate about, is that they ought to think about preparing for their funeral services. They ought to write down what they want from the funeral liturgy and reflect about what they would like from the service to ensure their life is celebrated and remembered. That exercise itself can be creative because it focuses people on the point that one day death *will* happen and that their lives are a journey to that point. And that by thinking about it now, they can have greater control and freedom in their lives.

One of the reasons I am a Christian, more than anything in the world, is that somehow that Christian theology – the life of Christ that God shares – says something profoundly unique about our wholeness and salvation being tied up with living our dying, dying to live. It asserts that if we're going to be free, we need to let go: and that there can be strength in our weakness. That the light and darkness, hopes and fears, our loves and hates, the separatedness and connectedness of our lives – all those paradoxes and contradictions – are somehow held together in Christ. He shows us what living our dying is about, and it gives us a hope, a truth and a purpose within both our lives and in our dying.

I'm not sure that I do cope very well in fact with all of these. My journey and struggle and pilgrimage continue. I'm sure that a part of my interest and work in this area is a continued inability to face fully my own dying. There's nothing resolved in my own life at the age of thirty-five about my dying. I've looked at it, thought about it, I experience it in other people's lives a lot, but I don't think that makes me any more resolved. It may be – and I need to face this possibility seriously – that part of my continued interest and work and conversation about the subject reflects my own unresolved feelings. I actually think that's true for a lot of people working in this area. Our professional work meets many of the needs we all have. The only point of resolution of those issues must be the point at which my physical body will breathe its last and I will die. The particular dialogue and struggle that goes on in my thinking, my practice and my writing is how my feelings relate to my thoughts and intellect. I am aware of a fairly consistent, personal pattern of behaviour which copes with some of the fearful feelings by intellectualizing them. At one level, all writing is therapy and a working out of something we haven't quite understood for ourselves. Therefore, there is a sense in which some of my work is a kind of therapy, and I think it's important to be honest and aware of that.

Fundamentally, I fear being out of control of the process of dying. I fear the letting go, the dependence, the pain of separation. I fear facing my inadequacies and failures – my failures in relationships, the times at which I have been the cause of pain and difficulty to others. There is a kind of judgement in death, where, if you allow it, you face aspects of your life as they truly are. In a very real sense I fear the point at which there will be judgement about who I am and what I've done. I know that it's not all bad! There is a lot that's been positive and creative, but in all human lives there is a shadow side which death and dying can bring to the surface.

Having worked in a hospital for nearly six years, with virtually every major physical condition under the sun, I do wonder what I might die from. Will it be a heart attack, cancer, renal disease, a car accident? I think my tolerance of physical pain is quite low and I do fear pain.

And there is so much that I still want to do. There is so much that is wonderful and beautiful about my life, and I don't want to let those things go.

The other thing I feel very ambivalent and agnostic about is life after death. I really am terribly unclear about all that. Some people think that it must be okay to do this kind of work because at least I have the faith to know that death isn't the end, and that this faith somehow makes sense of the suffering. I think that could easily be escapist. I am not saying that I think that death is the end, but I'm curious and sceptical about the kind of existence there is beyond death.

When I ask patients here what they think it will be like, the most common answer is that they will meet up with their loved ones. I think it's important though to be open about belief and how belief relates to practice. For example, this is demonstrated as one looks at the Christian funeral liturgy. I believe that liturgy and worship can reflect a rich diversity of belief in terms of what it shares with people about living and dying. If you look at the Anglican funeral service, it draws boundaries too sharply between those people who believe in

Jesus and have come to faith and those who don't share that particular perspective. There's a great deal of emphasis on the hope of things to come rather than on the things that have happened in a person's lifetime: the unresolved agendas that are part of all our living and dying. As an act of pastoral care, I don't believe the funeral liturgy is a very good model of caring for people in their grieving. It says quite difficult things about who God is and where God stands on boundaries about truth and salvation.

I think the attractiveness and the integrity of the tradition of Anglicanism, however, is that it is a tradition of Christian witness that has moved, developed, adapted and changed. The Church has always had to face controversy and disagreement and variance over opinions, thoughts and approaches to truth. Take a look at Paul's letters in the New Testament and the way he attempted to get communities to think through their disagreements and conflicts. Perhaps we have to continue to learn that being in conflict and disagreement is part of a healthy human existence and a healthy struggle with faith, hope and reality.

Having affirmed that, I am perturbed at aspects of the Church's inability to integrate some of its theological thinking and liturgical practice into the lives and concerns of what is happening to people in the world. Some of its thinking around what the Church is and what it does is intellectually shallow and theologically bankrupt. We're in danger of losing out by not engaging with the world as it is and listening to the concerns of people's lives.

Nowhere is this more glaring and challenging to the Churches than when we come to our understanding and practice around HIV disease and AIDS. I long for a creative dialogue and debate about issues around gender and sexuality as they relate to our spirituality. The Churches' position traditionally taken in relation to women, to physicality and sex is very ambiguous. These issues are complex areas of human contestation and conflict. I don't believe that the world is necessarily more resolved about these issues. The hospital here has an equal opportunities policy, but that doesn't mean women are treated equally as men. I think often the Church basically reflects the world's prejudices and difficulties. There is a judgement here. When historians look at what Christian theologians have said about AIDS and HIV, or what they've said about disease in general, they will find there has been judgement against the Churches' engagement with these issues. And I do what I can in my writing and practice to distance myself from aspects of the ways in which some Christians have responded to AIDS and HIV.

What these responses have crystallized is a very close parallel between disease and morality. Some of my work with the dying in this area has concerned itself with how we conceptualize what's going on, inviting them to think about the words we use and their meaning. Take, for example, the subject of AIDS/HIV: words do matter and there can be good and bad meanings to the words we use in relation to that particular disease. One has to be terribly careful about the nature and quality of moral judgement that's going on in the press. The way in which words are used.

When I was a curate in the north-east of England, I was a part-time hospital chaplain. There were several funerals within my parish and, despite my hospice experience, I felt quite ill-equipped to deal with some of the things that were presenting themselves. So I went on a counselling course, thinking this was going to provide me with the skills to engage with the challenges that confronted me in my work. I was further intrigued by what kind of framework and meaning psychology and counselling gave in terms of how this particular ideology understood humanity, both in relation to its appreciation of what went wrong with people and what the possible range of solutions was. I was particularly interested in the importance of suspending judgement if you are a counsellor. On the course I did a piece of work that explored how far counselling could operate as an activity without a sense of sin or wrong.

I became convinced that in our understanding and interpretation of life there can be no neutrality and that the operation of judgement is happening all the time. There are things in our human lives that are wrong and that need re-shaping – and that we therefore need some kind of forgiveness and absolution. I believed that counselling needed to have a boundary around which we understand that some things were acceptable and some things were not. Judgement is therefore not inherently bad or wrong – but the criteria by which judgements are made need to be carefully examined.

When I left the North-East to take a post in Oxford, I was very concerned at the way in which the Church was dealing with the AIDS/HIV issue. This was between 1987 and 1989. The aspect of the Churches' perspective on AIDS was that it was some kind of divine judgement on people who weren't monogamous heterosexuals. My interest was both intellectual and emotional – I felt this was a wrong meaning and needed to be put right. I was also emotional because I felt this awful sense of injustice. I didn't want to belong to a Church that marginalized people. I didn't want to belong to a Church that talked about God in the way that it did. I didn't want to belong to a Church that wanted to draw sharp boundaries between who was in and who was out. I didn't want to belong to a Church in which religion was used to hurt and alienate people.

So there was this kind of joining between an emotional and an intellectual agenda, as I said 'No, this will not do'. I didn't want to be a representative of a Church that talks about people like this. There was a lot of energy and a lot of anger. At that stage I didn't stand back and ask why I was getting so worked up, nor did I consider the fact that it was such a big issue – I just decided to do something about it. I registered for a research degree and did a piece of research on the Churches' understanding and representation of AIDS and HIV. I realized that few people were going to read this thesis and I needed to produce a piece of writing that would change people's hearts and minds. That was where the vision for *Embracing the Chaos* came from: to put together a book where good theology was informed by the stories of the lives of people affected by AIDS/HIV.

Something that I have understood from my experience here is that we do not particularly want to think about death and that we don't want to think about disfigurement and disease either. This is understandable. It's regarded as a weakness. In contemporary culture, we live with ideals where people are beautiful, slim, wealthy and successful. We don't deal with the reality and complexity of how we are, especially how we are on the inside.

So, take the combination of an incurable disease which is sexually transmitted and the result is a powerful combination of realities that are hard to get our heads and hearts around. I don't think anybody coped with it very well to begin with – there was a lot of panic and a lot of fear. I think it's been worked on and I think that's to everyone's benefit. There are many people living with HIV who have been significant in the transforming effect simply by sharing the story of their lives with others.

Inevitably, the attitudes within the Churches are still varied. Because the virus has not really entered the mainstream in the way that it has in Africa and other countries, it still continues to be a disease that predominantly affects gay men. So it's not just the disease that people are having to cope with; they're having to face and share other aspects of their private lives. One of the challenges facing the Churches is to develop a theology of sexuality. We need to come to terms with the relationship beween the private and the public in our lives. We need to learn how to deal with intimacy and difference, diversity and ambiguity in sexuality.

People with HIV/AIDS were really treated rather like

modern-day lepers; isolated from the rest of the human race. That has improved, but to go back to my point about the way we deal with the 'non-beautiful' in our culture, there are many other examples of this kind of marginalization. The way we deal with the elderly, for instance, is I think disgraceful. In a multi-cultural city like Birmingham, it is very moving to see how the Asian people attend to their older people with care and sensitivity. We have much to learn from one another.

I think that some of our attitudes – the fear of being close to these aspects of life – are partly bound up with not wanting to confront our own inner fears. We don't really want to know. Part of that is understandable, but it can also make for a very inhuman and fragmented society.

There is a kind of spiritual poverty that results from our fragmentation and disconnectedness. I think we're all the poorer as a society for it; I think we're all the poorer for not being able to integrate the reality of death as my family were all those years ago. The way we die these days must have something profoundly to do with the way we live. If we live busy, fragmented lives where we don't attend to difficult questions or challenging feelings, then our living and dying are bound to be messy and complex. We end up not even having a language in which to articulate what's going on. I think that the spiritual has become very marginal in our modern culture.

For example, I look at young people and the number of them who take recreational drugs. There is a danger in moralistic judgements, but there must be something about the persistent escapism through the use of drugs that is running away from what people are feeling. The galloping consumerism and the acquisition of material things must have something to do with a sense of emptiness inside – we acquire something to make us feel better. There is even the sense that we acquire relationships in order to escape an unbearable loneliness. Forgetting that whether you're in a relationship or not, life is lonely. That's just the way it is. We all have much to learn from exploring that inner geography of our hopes and fears: our common destiny. This is about cultivating depth and shape and colour in our lives; uncovering a sense of the spiritual that holds our lives together.

8

Dr Anthony Storr

Anthony Storr is a psychiatrist and author. His
publications include *The Integrity of the Personality,
Human Destructiveness, The Dynamics of Creation,
Solitude* and *Music and the Mind.* His most recent
work, *Feet of Clay,* takes a critical look at the role of
the guru in modern society. He is a Fellow of the
Royal College of Physicians, a Fellow of the Royal
College of Psychiatrists and a Fellow of the Royal
Society of Literature.

He is also a severe asthmatic. In 1969, at the age
of forty-nine, he had his first life-threatening
attack, during which he had an out-of-body experience. He has been close to death as a result of
asthma on a number of subsequent occasions.

I had asthma as a child, which I seemed to grow out of as many
people do between the ages of eighteen and twenty. I had no problems with it for several years, but it came back again in 1969. When
it came back, it came back severely. I wasn't used to dealing with it
in those days and I had one attack in December 1969, which was
extremely bad. I couldn't get hold of my doctor, through no fault
of his, and I was lying in bed, panting and struggling for each
breath. I remember thinking to myself that not only was this the
worst asthma attack I had ever had, but it was also the worst attack
I had seen as a doctor. Then I suddenly had the sensation of
becoming absolutely calm and of thinking, 'Well, this could go
either way – I might die from this.' I became completely detached

and calm and felt as if I was looking down on myself. I don't think I actually floated up to the ceiling, but it was as if I was looking down on my panting body. The interesting thing to me was how calm I was, that I wasn't distressed in any way.

In fact, when the doctor eventually did come, he was far more agitated and worried than I was. There was a terrific commotion, because I really was near death. Fortunately, however, he carried oxygen in his car and was able to give me intravenous injections and I recovered. People tend not to think of asthma as a potentially fatal disease, but there about two thousand deaths a year in this country.

After that experience, I rather rashly assumed that this might happen to a lot of people: that at the moment of death, or near death, something happens which cuts out the suffering and the anxiety, and I concluded that this was a wonderful protective device. It reminded me of the experiences which people have had in battle, where they've often had terrible wounds but have been quite unconscious of them. There obviously are ways of dissociating your physical experience from your mental experience. For at least a few moments, you can be quite unconscious of very severe trauma – rather like fainting when pain becomes intolerable.

Since that particular experience of mine in 1969, I've had other severe attacks, but never again that out-of-body sensation. At the time, I felt comforted by the idea that when I do come to die, it might be less alarming than I had supposed. I'm afraid, however, that since reading more about this subject – in particular one book by Sherwin Nuland called *How We Die* – I realize that that is a bit romantic. Many people do suffer and have a very unpleasant time, despite pain control. When I was a young doctor, I certainly saw people dying in great distress and I had no hesitation about giving them large doses of morphine.

I have no idea really why I had my particular experience. I think people vary greatly as to how much they live in their body and how much they dissociate. I suppose I'm someone who can dissociate easily: for example, if I'm busy thinking or writing, I don't always realize I'm sitting uncomfortably. I've known some writers who screw themselves up in uncomfortable positions and then complain of a back pain later, mainly because they were so preoccupied with their intellectual efforts that they were quite unconscious of their bodies.

Certainly I hope that when I do come to die, and I'm quite likely to die of some respiratory problem, I might be able to dissociate as I did in 1969. I rather hope that happens again.

I know some people develop strong religious beliefs after such an experience, but I haven't. I don't believe in an afterlife. I was brought up in a Christian family, in the shadow of Westminster Abbey in London in fact, but I ceased to be a believer in late adolescence, and I've been a non-believer since.

Had my life not been saved and I had entered further into death, I have no idea whether that calm sensation would have remained or what would have happened. These experiences very seldom last; they're rather like mystical experiences, which don't last either. I've also had the kind of experiences which people describe as mystical, but of course these don't have to be described in religious terms. Many people have wonderful, transcendental experiences when alone in contact with Nature: I've had those and they are some of the most beautiful experiences of my life, but I don't interpret them in religious terms.

I don't find these experiences easy to understand, but I think they're illusory. In many ways it's rather like being in love. That too is illusory in the sense that you don't see the person realistically. You have a completely idealistic picture, which must therefore be out of touch with reality. Freud called being in love 'the normal prototype of the psychoses', and I think he's right! It's a delusional state and we all have delusions from time to time. I don't mean to run it down because it's also a very valuable experience: it can lead onto a relationship and knowledge of another person, which you wouldn't get if you hadn't been in love. So even though the experience of being in love may not last, while it is there, it's enormously important.

We all have a number of experiences, which, if they were continuous and not intermittent, would be termed insanity. I don't think there is a great gap between the states of sanity and insanity, as some people believe: it's more like a sliding scale and we go up and down it. It's commonplace that we all have fluctuations of mood, but when these are excessive, it is called manic-depressive illness.

What's interesting is that we are discovering that many more people than we realized have the kinds of hallucinatory experiences that were once thought to be characteristic of schizophrenia. A lot of normal people keep quiet about these experiences, in case other people think they're crazy.

Death is another subject that people tend not to talk about. Perhaps people think about it more than we realize but keep their thoughts and feelings to themselves, in case others think they're crazy. One of the major characteritics of Western civilization at the moment is that we try to sweep death under the carpet. It's more indecent to talk about death now than it is to talk about sex. When death was an ever-present threat, as it was in Victorian times, I think people were much more open about it. If you look at some of the older customs of dealing with the dying you can see that much of the modern technology that surrounds death today can abolish the appropriate feelings. I remember reading a novel by the Greek author Kazantzakis about a death in a Greek village in the nineteenth century. An old man was dying, and towards the end he's taken to the village square and all his relatives come up to kiss him goodbye. I thought when I read it how much more sensible that was than the way we try to cover it up and pretend it isn't happening.

As a psychiatrist I've never treated someone at the time they were dying, but I've certainly talked to people who are dying and I don't pull any punches about it. You don't have to push it at people, but if they know they're dying and you know they're dying, I don't see that there should be any secret about it. In fact, I think it's much better not to make a secret of it.

I think we do have a cultural problem with denial; the impact of which is to leave people unprepared for death. There is one school of thought, for instance, that says we should think of death and our own dying every day. The ancient Egyptians arranged that a skeleton should be present at their feasts. The skelelton was brought in to remind the people that this life wouldn't go on for ever. I like to recall Jeremy Taylor's *Holy Living and Dying*:

> He that would die well must always look for death.
> Everyday knocking at the gate of the grave; and then the gates of
> the grave shall never prevail upon him to do him mischief.

When it comes to physical death, we face another cultural issue: the awful tendency to over-treat the dying. If someone has a terminal illness, they may want to die, and the idea of prolonging life at all costs, especially if it's a miserable life, is harmful. I think doctors can be over-anxious to intervene. They have these wonderful boxes of tricks and they want to use them. It is also diYcult for many of them to witness pain, although the training given to doctors to help them deal with pain is better than it was in my day. I remember noticing how little people were told, for example, about what was going to happen to them before an operation.

Perhaps one of the major problems underlying all of this is that of not knowing how to deal with loss. We have this English ideal of not showing our feelings. In other cultures, they beat their breasts and wail. This peculiarly British habit of pretending business as usual is just the worst thing to do. In my book *Solitude* I suggested that one of the functions of solitude is to aid mourning. I was in America soon after the book was published and I was taking part in a radio phone-in. One man rang in to say that he was very glad I had written the book because when he lost his wife, he had gone away entirely by himself for ten days to a place by the sea he'd never been to before – and he felt this had been absolutely the right thing to do. It gave him the chance to come to terms with the death of his wife in a way he never could have done if he'd tried to continue as normal.

I remember the time when I was a very young doctor, working in the London Hospital in Whitechapel, which in those days was largely occupied by Orthodox Jews. They had mourning customs whereby the person who had been bereaved wasn't allowed to go to work and was only allowed to go to the synagogue. Their meals were brought to them and people might come and be with them for a while, but the idea was that they had to experience this loss in all its depth and all its intensity. That way, you get over it much more quickly.

A lot of people who come into psychotherapy do so because they've never mourned something or someone properly, and when you touch on this, they burst into tears and feel terribly ashamed. They had not realized that a particular loss, which might have been several years previously, was still affecting them so much. I think that is because we try to sweep the impact of loss and of death under the carpet.

There is a link here between grief and insanity in fact. Some people don't want to face their feelings of loss, because they're afraid they will go mad if they do. They fear that the intensity of the feelings will push them over the edge. In fact this is a misinterpretation of the fear: the real fear is of losing control. I don't know of any instance where pain has made somebody go mad: it's not how mental illness develops, but obviously great distress can lead to loss of control. That isn't going mad. It's a perfectly normal reaction to distressing circumstances.

It's interesting to look at the meaning of words like 'hysterical'. What's understood by 'hysterical' in a technical sense by psychiatrists is not the same as what the ordinary person understands when they refer to hysterical screaming and shouting. Hysteria, in the Victorian past, was what some of Freud's patients were treated for: and many of these patients were simply women whose lives were intolerable. They were extremely frustrated, had very few outlets and so developed physical symptoms of various kinds, like paralysis, in order to draw attention to themselves and in order to get help.

Since the partial emancipation of women, you don't really see cases of 'grande hysterie' any more. Alice James, the sister of William James and Henry James, was a marvellous case in point. She was a chronic hysteric, but she was highly intelligent and creative, and in those days, in upper-class Boston, there was no outlet, there was nothing for her to do. Sewing classes were about all she could do. Furthermore, she was no beauty and was never going to get married – her whole life was intolerably frustrating.

Nowadays, it is depression that is the most common psychiatric problem. Depression is the major mental illness of our time. Yet, once again, when you look into the reasons why people get depressed, you can see that depression is often a perfectly natural reaction to circumstances in their lives! They may have been abandoned, they may have five children to bring up and not enough money – social factors come into it a great deal.

This is not in any way to deny that manic-depressive illness, recurrent depressive illness, chronic depressive illness are genetically determined and are inherited.

It is also true that the denial of death and the inability to deal with loss and separation may be contributing to the modern problem of depression. For example, people are more liable to develop severe depression if they have lost a parent, especially a mother, before the age of twelve. What brings on a severe depression is usually a combination of factors: factors which for the majority of people are minor provocations, but which for a vulnerable individual are devastating.

Yet, if we look at some of the most creative people in history, many of them were depressives – Virginia Woolf, Sylvia Plath, Robert Schumann, Vincent van Gogh. The strongest association between creativity and depression is found in fact in poets. Depression acts as a spur; if you tend to get severely depressed, you'll do anything to avoid getting into that state, and creating something is one way of preventing depression. It's partly to do with creating an imaginary world, which takes you out of the one you're actually living in.

This is true right down the whole scale of human behaviour. The fact is that we've always been inventive, and presumably that's because we're not entirely satisfied with what we've got. If you're an insect and are perfectly adjusted and you just act instinctively in relation to your environment, there's no reason to alter your behaviour. We are always dissatisfied and so constantly imagining something better. So, in a sense, the more dissatisfied you are, the more creative and inventive you will be.

If you were permanently in that state of blissful oneness I described earlier, you wouldn't do anything. You'd just be having a wonderful time! Maybe the act of looking for that state, however, does lead to creativity. If you take a musical composition, I think you can make out quite a powerful argument that that perfect work of music is creating an imaginary world in which everything is perfectly balanced. So, although in one sense this is an escape from the real world, in another it is also the creation of a world that is above ordinary existence.

My own creativity is probably fuelled more by a desire to avoid depression than to recreate a mystical experience. I'm someone of a depressive personality – I can get very depressed – and I'm sure that that's a spur to my writing in particular. Depression is in my family, but I've never been bad enough to be hospitalized or to have medication. I probably go down further than many people do and it can take me longer to get over it. But I find it helpful to keep on working, and so I'm sure that's exactly what I'll do right up until the end.

The end for me is pretty close. I find it extraordinary that I'm still alive at the age of seventy-six – the men in my family tend to die around the age of seventy – and considering how much I have wrong with me, I'm very surprised still to be here. I've been lucky, though: I've had extremely good doctors and a great deal of help from them. Nevertheless, I have the feeling that death could happen any day and I think I'm prepared for it. That's not to say that I feel as if I've lived my life in the way I would have wanted to – far from it – so perhaps I'll have to come back again. Let's hope that I don't come back as a donkey.

9

Roland Marshall

Roland Marshall is serving a life sentence for
murder. He is forty-six years old and it is thirteen
years since he committed his offence. The past four
and a half years of his sentence have been spent at
HMP Grendon. Grendon is a therapeutic community, which enables men to address their offending
behaviour with the use of individual and group
therapy. Inmates seek to change old attitudes and
values in order to return to society with a responsible and mature relationship to themselves and
others.

Roly was born in Germany and brought up in
England. He is one of four children, all of whom
were physically and sexually abused by their father,
who was later imprisoned for his offences.

Roly had several jobs after leaving school: he
worked as a civil servant, builder, painter, grounds-
man, press operator, car worker. He was in the
Royal Armoured Corps of the British Army. He has
been married three times and has two children: a
son from his first marriage and a daughter from his
second. He is now single.

I'm serving a life sentence for murder. In January 1984 I was living
in Grimsby; I'd moved into a council house not long after my wife
and I had split up and had been there about two months on my
own.

When I think about how I was then, I can only see myself as a selfish, ignorant, drunken bastard really. I had, and still have, a drink problem, and that will stay with me for the rest of my life. At that time my problem was severe and whenever I was drinking, that's when all the troubles started, and quite often people around me would get hurt. My wife left me for those reasons.

During that particular time I was feeling really sorry for myself, having spent Christmas on my own. I wasn't looking for revenge as such, but I felt I wanted to get out and have a good time and so I went out with that cock-sure, couldn't-care-less attitude. I wasn't actually aware of thinking like that, but that's what it was and I'd behaved like that dozens and dozens of times.

That particular day in January I'd gone into town and met a friend of mine and invited him to come out for a drink with me, to come and enjoy himself. We went round different pubs in Grimsby and at about 10 p.m. he asked if he could come back to my house. As we came out of the off-licence, he introduced me to my victim, although of course I didn't know that then. It struck me straightaway that my mate knew Wendy because she was staying at the Salvation Army Hostel. Both my wife and I had worked for the Salvation Army before and my mate's father was the Major in charge of the hostel. Unfortunately, I was of that macho opinion that any woman that stayed at that hostel was fairly low down the scale of morals, and my immediate opinion of her was pretty low. Her demeanour only made it worse – she'd been out drinking herself. It seemed quite reasonable to me at that time to mentally knock a woman down like that.

We all went home together and stayed up, drinking and playing music. Then my friend started touching her up and undressing her, and I was quite shocked, to tell you the truth. I'm not a prude but I was quite shocked and realized he knew her a lot better than I thought he did! I was also amazed that she was allowing this to happen in somebody else's house and in front of a complete stranger. But then I thought that I would get involved too and so I did. We were all mucking about – sexual tomfoolery you could call it. Her attitude confirmed my mental picture of her as someone who was beneath me.

Then my friend took her upstairs, and when he came down, he told me he'd hidden her clothes. I didn't know why he'd done this, but later I found out that it was because he was going to go out and he was offering her to me as a gift. At the time I didn't take a lot of notice; I just thought it was strange. Anyway, Wendy then came downstairs with my bed quilt wrapped around her and I just took it for granted that if she was prepared to let me do to her what I'd been doing earlier, she'd let me go upstairs with her. Which she did and we had sexual intercourse. My friend was still there when we came downstairs, but then he suddenly decided to go, which again I found strange. Normally he would stay the night whenever he came round. I realize now that he may well have been very angry about my behaviour towards Wendy, but because he was scared of me, he left the scene rather than complain and cause trouble for himself.

So Wendy and I were alone and we went upstairs to bed and had sex again. I'm sure now that this was not what Wendy wanted. She made no complaint I feel because she was scared of my reaction if she had said no. As I had not asked her and took what I wanted without any regard for her feelings, the sex we had was coerced and not consented to. I had mentally coerced her into sex for fear of the consequences if a refusal was aired by her. It's a kind of mental rape.

I'll always remember the bit just before the murder: my double bed sagged in the middle, and as I moved to get off her, I thought I must have pinched her skin because the next thing I know, she's clocking me round the head and starting to act very, very strange. Because I had her so low in my estimation, down with the animals, when she started lashing out at me I thought it was directed at me and I just thought: 'You bitch, you've been in my house, you've been drinking what I bought, everything's been okay here, and now you've had what you wanted, you're throwing a paddy against me.' I took it all personally, projected all my negative thoughts onto her – and lost my temper. I started to grab her round the throat and I almost throttled the life out of her, but that didn't seem to do anything. Unfortunately, when my wife had left me I'd got quite paranoid and I'd got used to carrying a knife round – and the knife was in the bed. In the course of the commotion on the bed, I saw the knife and, thinking 'this will stop you', I stabbed her. I stabbed her twice in the chest.

When I realized what I'd done, blind panic set in. I just totally panicked and realized how far I'd allowed myself to go. You think silly things; I remember thinking 'How can I mend this? How can I make this better again?' I really wanted to do that, I really wanted to stop the clock and take it all back again and do it another way. But I knew I couldn't do that and that hurt me badly. When I was sober I realized that the violence that was coming out was nothing I couldn't have controlled anyway – I'm a biggish lad and I could quite easily have controlled the situation, but I didn't. What controlled me totally were my emotions, the way I felt and not what was going on in somebody else.

During the panic I went from realizing I couldn't make it better to wanting to cover it up. Not wanting anybody to know it was me. I knew that was futile too. I'm not that overtly criminally minded. I didn't want to go and dig a hole, and I didn't fancy picking up a dead body; I just wanted to get away. I went downstairs, but the next thing I knew was waking up freezing cold on the settee. The first thought was whether it had really happened or not, but I knew it had. I grabbed what clothing I had and acted very methodically – I fed the dog, tidied up the downstairs and then went out. I fled.

I went into Grimsby, got on a train and went to Scunthorpe, went into a pub and had a few drinks. The whole thing is churning over in my mind and I can't get away from it – everything I was doing or looking at was bringing it back. I didn't know what to do: there were two lines of thought, the first was to commit suicide, to get away from it and because I deserved to be dead. But then I was too scared to harm myself. And so the other was to own up to it. I got back on the train to Grimsby, walked straight round to the police station and told them what I'd done. It was hard because I'd made friends with some of them during my work with the Salvation Army, but it was the best thing I've ever done in my life. It saved Wendy's parents having to go through all the fears of a missing daughter, not knowing what had happened. But it also saved me from the fear of continually looking over my shoulder.

In fact I'd always been the sort of person who would admit to doing things wrong, but I'd never done anything about it and never learnt from it. But here I'd done something so horrendous that it scared the life out of me and I had to do something about it. I had to change; to find out what made me the person I was, to understand the feelings I left others with, and what I could do to break the cycle and find better coping strategies.

What I didn't find out until months and months later was that Wendy was an epileptic and she had probably been going through a fit. And she was a violent epileptic, so much so that even her parents had restraining orders for her around the house because she would quite often go into fits and hurt her parents without meaning to. If it was a fit she was having with me, it could have been brought on by the unconsented sex or by her fear of me – or both. I know she is not to blame for any of this; I am to blame.

There is absolutely no justification for what I did. I was in the army and was trained to kill, and, as a young soldier, I thought there was some kind of justification in that. I don't justify taking anybody's life now. Actually, I didn't at the time of the murder really, but because of the sort of person I was, I used to justify everything I did and often blame others. To stop myself feeling too awful.

It isn't until I came inside that I began to realize where I'd been going wrong in my life – and the worst thing I did was to take Wendy's life. Looking back now I can see that what I did to her was the next step in an inevitable chain of events. If I think about the way I lived and acted, my value system, the way I used people as pawns – something like that was bound to happen.

I had so much crap that I carried around with me, and I hadn't resolved any of it. So, it was the people close to me, or who started to get close to me, that took it in the neck because that was easier than dealing with it myself. My life tended to be huge peaks and troughs: I would get out of these huge depths of despair and anger and pull myself up really high and get good jobs, promotions, and do very, very well. Then all of a sudden the fear and self-doubt – 'I'm not going to be able to do this because Dad always said I was a thick, ignorant pig; I'm not going to be able to cope with this; I'm going to make a mistake' – and if it didn't happen that way, I'd self-destruct. I'd make it happen. I didn't feel I was good enough to be up there, and then it would all come tumbling down; if there was someone in my life close to me, normally that relationship would break up. I'd been married three times and lived with two or three women as well, but I would always engineer the break-up of that relationship and justify it by saying that it was the other person's fault.

I used to think about death sometimes before the offence, but my thoughts were mainly about the death of my father, which is what I wanted when I was younger. That's what all four of us children wanted when we used to talk amongst ourselves. On the surface our home life was excellent – everything was there materially and we had a beautiful home – but it was what was going on in the home that wasn't right. We didn't want to plot to murder him or anything like that, but we used to dream of Dad not being there. I think the worst we ever thought was what if Dad had a car accident and didn't come back.

The only other time I thought about it much was when I went out to Aden with the army – there was action out there and I got a bit scared. I knew I was going to be shot at with real bullets and we weren't playing games any more. When I was shot at, I remember thinking how real it was and I didn't want to be there any more. But somehow the army instils in you this camaraderie and you know that if you run away, the other guy's going to get it in the neck and you don't want to be seen as a wimp, so you get over the blind panic, put a lid on it, and you churn away underneath – you know, you get the old diarrhoea and sickness, but you stay there. You try to look macho, but really you want to be little again with your mum there to comfort you. The fear comes out as aggression and you hurt innocent people.

Many a time I've done what millions of people do every day of their lives and said to myself, 'You bastard, I'll kill you.' You say that as a figure of speech without really meaning it – what you mean is you want to blot someone out of your life at that particular time because they're hurting you. I've never fantasized about killing anybody ever. I've fantasized about hurting them, I've got to be honest there, and I've fantasized about being far stronger than I am. Don't get me wrong, murderers aren't necessarily strong people just because they've taken a life. It doesn't take a lot of courage to kill somebody – in fact it doesn't take any at all.

Most of my death issues have been fears about the death of myself. I got to the stage on several occasions when I contemplated suicide: I'd got myself in such a rut, I couldn't see any way out, and I was always on this cycle. Every time I seemed to break away from it, I'd find myself back on it again; I never seemed to realize it was me causing this cycle.

I don't know whether I feared death, mainly because I tried not to think about it. I suppose I had a healthy respect for it. I would never cross the road without looking where I was going, for instance. Mind you, I've had a few fights and I've put myself in situations where if I'd gone one step more, somebody could have killed me. I've been in the wrong company, and some of the people I knocked around with once or twice in my life were not averse to doing something to you.

The trouble with murder is that people want a clear-cut answer. There isn't a clear-cut answer, because like everything in your life, it's a culmination of lots of emotions happening all at the same time. It's very much like a pyramid effect: you've got everything all the way through the pyramid until it reaches the point, and then the next step has to be off, and you've gone too far. Looking back at my offence, I remember there was of course anger and the need for some kind of revenge, but not necessarily revenge against the person I killed. Revenge for all the past grievances I'd never been able to cope with. I know this sounds contradictory, but really in a lot of ways, you're also stabbing yourself. You're doing it to yourself as well. At the time you're not thinking these things; all you want to do is get out of that situation. I wanted to get away from this thing I saw manifesting itself, which I saw as anger, hate; I wanted it to shut up and be quiet, and I knew I had the power to make it do that. There was no rational thinking, no realization that I could do this in a more logical way – just getting off the bed and letting her go through the fit, even if I didn't know that it was a fit she was having.

I've thought a lot about what I've done and of how the relatives of my victim feel. I don't really know if anything I can say or do can make it any better for them, if anything any murderer can do can make it better for their victim's family. For the first few years of my sentence, all I did was work on myself. Where was I coming from, where was I going to, and all the different stages in between: that's basically what I was looking at with psychologists, probation officers, etc. Why was I feeling these feelings at certain times? What could make me angry? How could I cope with that anger? How could I control it and channel it into another more positive way?

Even though I was very much aware of the victims – of Wendy's family and of my own – I still had to work on myself, otherwise how was I going to be able to understand anybody else's feelings? Then when I was in the eighth year of my sentence, I came here to Grendon. I was in a relationship by that time with a woman, whom I later married, whom I'd met while I was at Fulsutton: I'd started a magazine there and I'd asked Shirl, who was the Director of Aftermath, to do an interview for me. Aftermath is an organization that looks after the wives and families of long-term serving prisoners, especially lifers. Before that, she had worked with the victims of murderers. It was through talking to her more than anything else that got me onto that track – I started looking at the victims that I had caused within my own family. My Dad died about a year after I committed my offence, but I was still in contact with my mother who lived in Germany. I found it very, very hard to explain it all to her. How do you explain to your parents why you committed this kind of offence?

As I got more involved with Shirl, I began to meet some of her clients who would come down and visit us. I started then to think about my victim's family – what are they going through? What kind of feelings are they still left with? One of the things that always struck me is that they must always ask themselves why. Why? What happened and how did it happen and who was to blame? Very often they're not told what happened. Then all of a sudden it starts to hit home, because once you start thinking about them, you try to empathize and put yourself in their place. You can't do it totally, but what I used to do was to feel the pain and the hurt of what happened to me and mentally increase that a hundredfold to try to experience a little bit of what that family was going through. The only thing they won't let you do is contact your victim's family.

I know people do get over these things, inasmuch as they try to box it off and live a normal life; they try to muddle through even though things constantly remind them. But I couldn't think like that, I had to realize that maybe this family couldn't do that – maybe it had been such a horrendous blow to them that it had shattered their whole life. There could have been a divorce within their own family, because differences over what I've done may have broken relationships up. That's what happened to my family. Once the whole truth came out, the whole family practically split apart.

It sounds awful to say, but in some ways coming to prison was the best thing that could have happened to me. I've learnt so much about people and their feelings since I've had to deal with it all. I had no education before and I've done a degree and got a post-graduate diploma with the City and Guilds. One of the things I always say to the new guys who come on the wing is that here you suddenly realize that you go through most of your life with blinkers on. That's especially true for people who commit crimes because they're selfish people. You only see what's directly in front of you; if I'd been talking to you in the past, I would deal with you when you were there, but the minute I turned my head you'd be out of my vision. And I could be doing something that was hurting you emotionally, but because I'm not aware of you, why should I worry? It's as if you're a non-person. It can happen in a crowded room – you can be so intent on saying something to the person in front of you that you don't realize you're hurting somebody on the other side of the room. One of the things education has done for me, that Grendon has done for me, is that it's gradually enabled me to take these blinkers back and I can see the world in a much bigger way. I can see the ripples in the pond and how far they go out, when they hit obstacles. You've got to look at the little things as well, like when I upset my brother and sister when we were younger. Or when I let down an employer when he was really relying on me and I didn't turn up to work because I'd been too drunk the night before.

Then you think of the bigger things – the violence, the petty crimes. And then the murder. I started to realize that whatever I do in my life, I've got to be very aware, because everything I touch, everything I do or say affects someone else and reflects on me. It doesn't mean I'm walking on eggshells all my life; it makes me more realistic. And it doesn't mean I'm perfect – I still get a bit angry at times, I still feel the pangs of jealousy and envy. But they're normal feelings and I don't fear having them any more. I used to feel it was quite abnormal to have all those awful feelings and that I musn't have them.

Prison's been a good thing for me, but it's too late to bring Wendy back. I can't bring her back ever. I can't do anything about the past, but I can do something about the future.

10

Barbara McNulty

Five years ago Barbara's partner, Joan, began to show the first symptoms of Alzheimer's disease. Progressive brain deterioration has been described as a form of 'living death': memory loss and personality changes chip away at a person's identity until very little of the original person is left.

Barbara McNulty is a former nurse. She trained during the last war, leaving to get married in 1942. After many travels in Africa and Europe she returned to England to live, with her two children, as an oblate of a Benedictine Community in Prinknash. When she returned to nursing, she became interested in the care of the dying and in 1967 became one of the first ward sisters at St Christopher's Hospice. In 1969 she started the Home Care Service.

In 1978 Barbara left nursing and trained as a counsellor. She and Joan moved to a remote cottage in Wales, where they lived until Joan's condition became unmanageable. The couple now live in Bath, in accommodation with care facilities at hand.

It must be about five years ago that I began to worry about Joan. She'd had two or three major car accidents, and it was her response to those that seemed to me less than normal. They were tossed off with a sort of 'funny-ha-ha'. She was also constantly forgetful, which she said was just academic absent-mindedness. I became increasingly concerned, but the doctor kept saying I was imagining things. Joan appeared absolutely normal to people, but I began to get more and more suspicious.

Then two years ago she had a brain scan which showed certain brain changes, but they weren't very definite and people were still telling me she was absolutely fine. Socially, she presents an extremely good face and no one would guess that there was anything really wrong if you only saw her for a short while, or the conversation was superficial, or on her own subject. It's only when you see the day-to-day problems that you begin to realize things are not the same.

Joan's driving became more and more erratic; she also began to lose things constantly. She used to laugh at me and say 'This is my Alzheimer's'. Big joke. It didn't even occur to her that it could be real, whereas I was beginning to feel anxious and fearful; but I too didn't really want even to consider it; it became like a joke between us – 'you and your Alzheimer's'.

Then a year ago she had another brain scan at my insistence, and it did show further changes, shrinking of the cortex, not connected to those seen before. At that point I really felt we had to move because a country cottage in Wales with absolutely no communication at all, three miles from the nearest town, was getting too dicey; when the weather was bad, there was no access. So we began looking around.

I was sent a flyer about this place –Avonpark – which at the time was still being built. We liked the sound of what they promised, which was independence with help available twenty-four hours a day if necessary. And when I came up to have a look at this flat, it seemed the right move to make.

I was a hospice nurse for many years, but I have never had the care of anyone close to me who was dying, apart from my eldest child. He died when he was three. Caring for someone with

Alzheimer's is very different: to begin with, you don't want to believe that the person in front of you is actually changing. It's not like a physical illness, where you can see a body getting thinner, or a leg wasting away, or the hair falling out. There's nothing to see. So you're in constant doubt and uncertainty, which I don't think you are once a diagnosis of, say, cancer is made. You know where you are with cancer, you know how long it's going to go on for and what to expect. It's important to have a diagnosis with some idea of prognosis.

The difficulty for me is that I was never as close to any of my patients as I am to Joan – she's part of my life, and I know her almost as well as I know myself. I knew my patients well and we were often close, but although I would grieve with the families, I was never cut to the heart as I am at watching the disintegration and destruction of a personality that I'm very fond of. She's not the same person any more, and that I find is the most difficult thing to face.

Joan was a highly intelligent person with considerable insight. She has some insight now. Previously if she had told me that she wasn't feeling too good that week, but she knew she was okay, I'd have believed her. If she says that to me now, I know it isn't okay, and that the person who used to speak like that doesn't exist any more. It sounds so terrible, but I find I can't believe anything she says, because at the back of my mind I know she doesn't know how to assess, how to judge, how to weigh, how to contrast, or how to draw conclusions. For someone who had such a brilliant mind, it's so cruel.

I can't rely on her at all now and haven't been able to for over a year. She wants to help and to do things – 'I'll do it, don't worry. I'll do it.' But a week later, it'll still be there, still undone. Because she's forgotten. There might be a bag of garbage that needs to be taken downstairs and she's intending to take it down, but unless she actually sees it again, it won't enter her head, and even if she does see it, she might not recognize it for what it is. That's what I mean by disintegration of the personality.

There's always some depression with any illness, and she does get very depressed, when she realizes that she's just about to rush into the room to tell me something and it's gone. Gone completely. She might sit down with an idea she wants to write, she picks up her pen – and it's gone. That is frustrating beyond words and it's accompanied by depression. But in Joan's case, the depression is counterbalanced by excessive joy and happiness, an exaggerated 'high'. Huge swings of mood up and down: from seeing the beauty and loveliness of everything, feeling that this is a *wonderful* life and this is the best time of her life, to absolute rock bottom, when she feels it's not worth living and she wants to put herself into the canal at once. The mood can swing from one minute to the next.

I was totally unprepared for this. I'd never met anyone with Alzheimer's or even read about it. It sounds silly, but one becomes so narrowly focused on the type of palliative care you have with cancer that nothing else exists. You begin to think that everybody is dying of cancer.

Here in Bath, I have been very fortunate in finding a centre where they are doing research into memory problems, in particular those associated with Alzheimer's. I was asked if I would like to join a group of carers – I'm a great group joiner! – so I did. After a while, I began to hear other people's stories, and the amusing thing was that as people were talking about their various relatives or loved ones, I found myself thinking, 'Gosh, they're much worse than you are. That really sounds terrible.' Then last Christmas, we had a party and people came with their 'appendages', and I sat and talked to one or two of them and realized they were just like Joan! That was quite a shock to me. In fact Joan wasn't always sure which was the patient and which was the carer: she was talking to one man she thought had a brilliant mind and they were having a wonderful conversation – and he was the patient!

Joan's understanding of what's happening is limited. She knows she's forgetful and yet she doesn't connect it with the typical behaviour of people with Alzheimer's. She'll say to me: 'When I get like that ....', and I think 'But you *are* like that. You already are.'

When you realize someone you love has Alzheimer's, it's rather too much to take in all at once. At the group I was introduced to books, and I read a few, but then found it too much and stopped. However, now I'm starting again, because I do need to know more, but it has to be taken in stages. My own acceptance is also a gradual process.

In some ways I'm not sure how good it is to know *too* much, because I find I'm in danger of looking for things when they're not actually there yet. I have to be careful. Because it is also true that at one level she can be scintillating company, fun, amusing, chatty, open. Mostly – if you say the wrong thing, you can be sent out with a flea in your ear.

I find I go up and down quite a lot too. When I first had to leave Wales, it felt like the total loss of life – of my life, and I went through a very bad depression. I was so busy thinking about Joan's life that I hadn't looked at my own. When I went to see the GP because of my high blood pressure, she looked at me and asked if I was depressed. I burst into tears and said 'Yes, I am'; that was my first recognition of how painful it was and of how I was going through the various stages of grief.

I find the infinite sadness of watching the bit-by-bit destruction the hardest to bear. That the person I have known and loved isn't there any more – that is so crushing. That is something I cannot share with Joan. I can't share such feelings, because she's very dependent upon me and so my strength is essential. I feel it would be cruel to burden her with my sadness when she can't cope with her own.

My own feelings swing from one thing to the other. I'm indignant and angry – why should the Lord give me this problem now? It isn't what I wanted; I wanted to rest now. I *am* angry and resentful. I suppose because I have no life of my own, and my whole life is entirely bound up with Joan's needs. There isn't any space for me at all, but I'm trying to make some now. Everybody tells you that you've got to find time for yourself, you've got to get away. It's all very well to tell you, but try getting away from a limpet or an octopus. Try getting away. You can't. There's a kind of emotional blackmail, which is quite subtle: 'Why do you need to go away? I don't need to go away. We've always gone away together. You don't need to go away without me – why should you?' I try to explain, but there's no understanding in the way that there once would have been.

She is afraid, yes. When she stops to think about it. She has an unquestioning nature in many ways, totally unmedical – no understanding at all! She's an academic; her subject is the sixteenth century and that's where she lives. That's where she's alive. Nevertheless, she knows intellectually where she's going. We had a psychologist here the other day and Joan was going round in circles. She had asked me to tell her if she repeated herself, and I never know whether I should or not, because you're damned if you do tell her and damned if you don't. On this occasion, after Joan had told the same story three times, I said that we had actually talked about that. 'No, I haven't. Have I?', she said, and turned to the psychologist, who said yes, she had. Now that's a hard slap up against something: she can always disbelieve me and think I'm making it up, but when there's a third party … that was quite a shattering blow for her. 'I *am* going dotty,' she said.

The fear is not just to do with specific things; it's the loss of control. We all like to feel we've got some control over our lives. In fact none of us has as much control as we like to believe, because life has a way of taking you and rolling you along, but at the same time, there are many choices and decisions we make ourselves. But with this illness, there's no such control. You can't say that you won't be unkind, you won't lose your temper again – it's bad enough without Alzheimer's, but with it, you have *no* control. We've laughed about people who go out with odd socks on, but Joan does it too. She'll go out with odd shoes, or the wrong hand-bag – it's happening.

It's like having a six- or seven-year-old child: constant reassurance, constant affirmation, constant supportive loving. And if you've had the sort of relationship where you could talk about anything, share anything, then you have to face the loss of that. You can't talk any more. You're isolated. You're living in one house, but it's as though there is a great big iron curtain between you. And we haven't met the really difficult bits yet – I'm told by the books that those come later. I can't imagine what it'll be like. Somehow we'll get by and cope with that experience.

It isn't that the love goes. It changes. For me, it has become more protective, much more compassionate. So the whole rela-tionship has changed and it's not a peer relationship any more. It is more like a mother–child relationship.

I don't feel I cope very well at all. I do have support: I have the group at the hospital, the Alzheimer's Society group, friends and a sister. Down at Avonpark, there are always one or two people who will invite me to stop and have a cup of tea. I try not to worry them, but sometimes I need to.

The hard thing is that there's no way out of this. I remember when I took my first baby home from hospital, I thought then, 'I want out of here'. But you can't. And it's a 24-hour responsibility. In fact I remember reading a book called *The Thirty-Six Hour Day*, and it's damned right – you can get thirty-six hours into twenty-four.

I said earlier that one of the great benefits of Avonpark is that you can get help any time of day or night. I've begun to do that. A girl comes in for an hour or two in the morning every now and then. I want Joan to get used to the idea that somebody else is coming in, that I'm not always here, and I want her to know someone else well enough to trust them.

The line that I have drawn is that when Joan doesn't know me any more, and when she doesn't know where she is any more, she will go over to the main care centre. Because then I can't cope. Until then, I'll try. If it becomes too difficult from a nursing point of view, there is the nursing home and she knows there may come a time when she has to go somewhere like that. There's also the possibility of having 24-hour nursing care in the home. So we're very lucky really.

I get little notes written to me, frequently. The last one was: 'Don't let them resuscitate me. I don't mind an autopsy – I want to know what was there. I don't want any tubes or any special treatments. I don't want to be sent away except to here. Be sure to give my family and friends the choice of my books.' The latest thing we've been doing is planning her funeral: who is to take it, where will it be. Perhaps if we've crossed all these bridges, we shan't have to do it again.

Generally speaking, people die their own deaths and they are the kind of people that they are. They're not going to change radically in the last week or two of their lives. There is a potential in everyone for growth, and preparing for death must include the encouragement of this potential. Joan believes that too: that if she can prepare in her inner self, psychologically as well as spiritually, for anything, then even when her conscious memory has gone, something will remain to support her. I think that will be true. She will run true to her own inner form; nothing will change radically. The good parts of her will remain good and the not-so-good parts probably stronger. She sometimes worries whether she'll become violent. She is violent in word of mouth, but not physically. She has a cheerful, happy outlook on life and, although she gets depressed, that outlook is predominant.

She believes in life after death. She had a very reassuring dream a while ago; of going into a conference where there were a lot of people around her. There were a lot of strangers and it was all rather frightening and anxious-making. Then she suddenly saw, 'over the other side', lots of people that she knew – her grandmother, who was very influential in her life; her mother, who had died when she was quite young; her father and various other members of her family. And they all came forward and stretched out their hands to her. I think that is a wonderful dream, because that is where she is in her inner self – knowing that they will be there to greet her and that it's all okay. She doesn't have to fear that, and all I have to do is support her in the meantime, until she gets there.

I don't know whether you know *The Dream of Gerontius*, but there is a very strong bit at the beginnning of that when the soul cries to its friends, 'Pray for me, my friends, who can no longer pray'. I think that's an important role for all friends – to give support in prayer for those who can no longer do it for themselves. That's how I see my role. But don't think I feel strong about it, because I don't. All I feel is a big struggle.

I hadn't really appreciated the slowness of bereavement and that it has to be done again and again. You never get it 'done'. That is probably true even after a death – you don't get bereavement done. That is what I suspect, because I can see now how a year ago I was profoundly bereaved by the change in circumstances and of leaving behind what we had. The process repeats itself and there is this ongoing painful cycle of grief. At different depths each time. With every new development, there is a mourning.

I grieve for myself, of course. But I also grieve for Joan's loss – for the loss of all the life that might have been. I told you earlier that the only close person I've lost was my son, who was only three when he died. And although I've done a lot of work on it, on the feelings of loss, I can feel that acutely. It's as if each new bereavement reawakens an old one – and you just never get it finished. I know all about working through the feelings, but I don't believe that with a really profound grief you ever really 'heal'. You're always vulnerable.

I'm not going to let it get me down. One is called to live life as awarely as possible. As a young person, certainly up until my thirties, I think I was simply bowled along by life. Things came at me, and I don't believe I really made any decisions at all. I was totally unaware and in a kind of dream world, blissfully unconscious. Now it's important not to be just bowled along. I want to know what's happening and to be conscious. I now believe that everything that happens to us, that anyone who crosses our path, forms part of the pattern, is part of a bigger picture – one that consciousness, however painfully realized, can help us to see.